RUD(
philos
of the human being'. As a highly developed seer, he based his work on direct knowledge and perception of spiritual dimensions. He initiated a contemporary and universal 'science of spirit', accessible to anyone willing to exercise clear and unprejudiced thinking.

From his spiritual investigations Steiner provided suggestions for the renewal of many activities, including education (both general and special), agriculture, medicine, economics, architecture, science, philosophy, religion and the arts. Today there are thousands of schools, clinics, farms and other organizations involved in practical work based on his principles. His many published works feature his research into the spiritual nature of the human being, the evolution of the world and humanity, and methods of personal development. Steiner wrote some 30 books and delivered over 6000 lectures across Europe. In 1924 he founded the General Anthroposophical Society, which today has branches throughout the world.

DAILY CONTEMPLATIONS

Wisdom and Love

An Almanac for the Soul

RUDOLF STEINER

Compiled and edited by Jean-Claude Lin

RUDOLF STEINER PRESS

Translated by Matthew Barton

Rudolf Steiner Press,
Hillside House, The Square
Forest Row, RH18 5ES

www.rudolfsteinerpress.com

Published by Rudolf Steiner Press 2021

Originally published in German under the title *Weisheit und Liebe* by Rudolf Steiner Verlag, Basel, 2011. This translation is based on the second edition, 2018

© Rudolf Steiner Verlag and Jean-Claude Lin 2011
This translation © Rudolf Steiner Press 2021

All rights reserved. Apart from any fair dealing for the purpose of private study, research, criticism or review, as permitted under the Copyright, Designs and Patents Act, 1988, no part of this publication may be reproduced, stored in a retrieval system, or transmitted in any form or by any means, electronic, electrical, chemical, mechanical, optical, photocopying, recording or otherwise, without the prior written permission of the copyright owner. Inquiries should be addressed to the Publishers

A catalogue record for this book is available from the British Library

Print book ISBN: 978 1 85584 590 9
E-book: 978 1 85584 621 0

Cover by Morgan Creative
Typeset by Symbiosys Technologies, Vishakapatnam, India
Printed and bound by 4Edge Ltd, Essex

CONTENTS

Introduction	1
January	3
February	37
March	69
April	105
May	137
June	171
July	203
August	237
September	271
October	305
November	339
December	371
Sources	405

When the human being warm in love
gives himself as soul to the world,
when our being in bright and clear reflection
takes to itself the spirit from the world,
then in spirit-illumined soul,
in spirit that is soul-sustained
our spiritual being will truly be revealed
within our bodily being.

Rudolf Steiner
Berlin, 10 December 1915

INTRODUCTION

'Wisdom is the premise, the foundation of love; love is the fruit of wisdom reborn in the I.' With these words Rudolf Steiner concluded the first edition of his *Occult Science, an Outline*, published in 1910. While he added a few 'Details from the Domain of Spiritual Science' and some 'Supplementary Notes', this 'summation of anthroposophy'—as he called his *Occult Science* in 1925, shortly before his death, by and large ends with these words about wisdom and love. In the same way we find wisdom and love also as the founding motifs of his immense and manifold lectures: they are the alpha and omega of the human being who strives for truth and freedom.

In the following pages, passages by Rudolf Steiner have been chosen to accompany each day of the year. They are all taken from lectures or addresses that he gave on the day in question. Thus the ordering of these utterances does not originate, as is often the case in an almanac, with the volume's editor, but arises from the historical fact of the lectures themselves. The editor has of course decided which particular passages to select for this book.

In many cases I could have chosen a different text, either from the same lecture or from other lectures given on the same day of the month but in a different year. I am pleased that I was able to find passages for each day of the year which seem to me, at least, to have the right tenor. But there were also lectures that escaped my attention. It is perfectly possible that I might eventually make changes here or there, and therefore I make no claim to any general or ultimate validity of this selection. But I hope that it will encourage readers themselves to delve and reflect further, and to make their own creative discoveries.

I first formed the idea of this 'soul almanac' of comments by Rudolf Steiner at Epiphany 1987. But it was not until September 1999, in a conversation with Hannelore Roder following a lecture by Florian Roder on the clairvoyant power of faith, that this idea gained greater shape. I then embarked on a more detailed conception and realization of the book. I wish to thank her most warmly for this conversation and her firm encouragement.

Everything that Rudolf Steiner developed and created as an outcome of his experiences in the spirit was orientated to *life*: to help people take hold of their lives in ever more autonomous and creative ways for their own benefit and that of their fellow human beings. It is with this in mind that I gratefully dedicate this book to friends travelling the paths of truth and life, especially to Peter Wege and to my companion in life and inward endeavour, Susanne Wege.

Jean-Claude Lin
Stuttgart, Epiphany 2011

January

1 January

From wisdom rightly understood, virtue rightly understood will indeed be born in the human heart. Let us strive for true understanding of world evolution, let us seek wisdom; and then assuredly love will appear as the child of wisdom.

Hanover 1912, GA 134

2 January

Consider, if you will, that a significant impulse, a significant idea, needs 19 years to be fully and inwardly encompassed and understood.

Leipzig 1914, GA 266

3 January

Two sayings can guide us, can be extraordinarily important for us. The first of these, which we should inscribe deeply in ourselves, is this: *Strive for thought's death in the universe.* You see, only if a thought dies into the universe does it then become a living power outside us. And yet we cannot unite ourselves with this living power if we do not take heed of the content of the second saying: *Strive for destiny's resurrection in the I.* If you accomplish this, then you unite what is reborn in thought with the I resurrected outside you.

Dornach 1915, GA 275

4 January

To someone who regards it imaginatively, the whole rainbow reveals a streaming forth of the spirit, then a vanishing of the spirit. Wonderfully, it does indeed reveal something like a rolling spiritual cylinder. And at the same time we can see that as these spirit beings emerge, they do so in great fear, and as they enter in again, they do so with an unconquerable courage. If you look at the red-yellow region of the rainbow, fear streams forth from it. If you look at the blue-purple region, you gain the sense that everything of the nature of courage dwells there.

Dornach 1924, GA 233a

5 January

The teacher led the pupil out again, and, before taking leave of him, said: The human being of today and the earth of today are in such little accord with each other that you must receive the revelation of religion from the spirit of your own youthfulness high upon the mountains above the earth, and the revelation of nature from deep under the earth, in the crevasses below the earth's surface. And if you succeed in illumining with the light that your soul has drawn from the mountain what your soul has felt in the deep chasms of the earth, then you will come to wisdom. You see, in this form—I am speaking of the time around the year 1200—the deepening, the fulfilment of the human soul's wisdom was accomplished.

Dornach 1924, GA 233a

6 January

And behold, three from the group of those gathered there were truly destined to forge a special bond with the world of spirit, not by some kind of mediumistic powers but by development of that mystic, meditative, pious mood. And these three, who were then specially protected by the others of the group, really inwardly nurtured, sometimes experienced a kind of absence. Their outward corporeality was wonderfully beautiful, they acquired something like a shining countenance, sun-luminous eyes; and during this time they wrote symbolic revelations that they received from the world of spirit. These symbolic revelations were the first images in which the Rosicrucians were shown what they should know about the world of spirit. These symbolic revelations contained a kind of philosophy, a kind of theology, a kind of medicine. And the remarkable thing was that the others—and it seems to me as if there were four others, so that together there were seven—were able to reproduce in ordinary speech what they had experienced as the meaning of the symbols in the sun-luminous eyes, the shining countenance, of their three brothers. The brothers destined to draw forth these symbols from the world of spirit were able only to inscribe them. When they returned to their ordinary state of consciousness again, they were able to say only that they had walked amongst stars and star spirits, and had found there the ancient teachers of esoteric knowledge. They themselves were not able to couch these symbolic images, which they drew, in ordinary human language. But the others were able to do so and did.

Dornach 1924, GA 233a

7 January

If we are to try to understand Christianity in a manner that accords with the most contemporary needs of humanity, then we will have to penetrate it with the spirit which hitherto has only pervaded natural science, with all its social consequences, through the powers of the West. In any worldview drawn from these powers of the West, people are not content unless they can formulate it in clearly detailed and sharply outlined concepts. For the future of the earth, human beings will need such clear and sharply outlined concepts.

Dornach 1922, GA 210

8 January

The Western world has fewer traditions. Only in the chronicles of certain secret Orders does it retain traditions from the third post-Atlantean cultural epoch, the age of cosmosophy—yet these are traditions that are no longer understood but rather are presented to humanity in uncomprehended symbols. Here in the West, however, there is at the same time an elemental power capable of unfolding new evolutionary impulses.

Dornach 1922, GA 210

9 January

Today I gave you an example of how we can develop a schema like this from the lecture cycles. I hope that many of you will gradually come to develop such schemas for yourselves. Then, firstly, insubstantial speculation about the content of the cycles will grow less, and that is a very good thing; and secondly, through such compilations and configurations, you can really undergo processes of inner evolution. Individuals will make progress if they compose these kinds of fruitful compilations. Besides just combining a few such passages from the cycles, you can render fruitful the material contained in the cycles by juxtaposing and combining not only hundreds but many, many thousands of passages, perhaps even more.

Dornach 1915, GA 161

10 January

A wonderful example of how you can allow anthroposophy to enliven you is to be found in the beautiful poem 'Lucifer' by our dear Christian Morgenstern—a poem which, it seems to me, lives fully in the atmosphere of feeling that I tried to hint at today, which can attend our efforts to pass on from the ideas of anthroposophy to the grasping of living beings.

> My light from yours I wish to hide away,
> I do not want you, me you shall not enjoy
> until my own light brightly I have kindled.
>
> And I bring evil thus to manifest being
> as separate spirit, spirit of negation,
> yet my spirit order creates new world.
>
> At odds with beings who never leave the fold,
> a line of gods in error will unfold
> who make their own—not your—resolves;
>
> who do not walk in truth from the beginning,
> but only gain truth at last through suffering,
> who suffer the truth they gain through their own action.

Dornach 1915, GA 161

11 January

Many violent expressions of human nature, especially those that come close to being pathological, would be avoided if people were less forgetful.

Munich 1912, GA 143

12 January

Interpreting symbols is really nonsensical. All nit-picking deliberation about their meaning is nonsense. The right way to relate to symbols is to make them, to experience them; and in the same way we ought not to absorb fables, legends and fairy tales with the merely abstract intellect but should identify ourselves with them.

Dornach 1924, GA 233a

13 January

It is true to say, my dear friends, that, having experienced the Rosicrucian principle of initiation as it is here intended, and then studying the tenets of Haeckel with all its materialism, studying this and imbuing yourself with methods of knowledge as given in *Knowledge of the Higher Worlds*, then the following will occur. If you read Haeckel's *Anthropogeny* about human ancestors, learn about this though you may find it distasteful, learn everything about this subject which you can gain from outward science, then bear it upward to the gods, you will arrive at the nature of evolution as described in the book *Occult Science*... And what we do here by taking scientific tenets, or also works of naturalistic art, or also the sentiments of a religion that works naturalistically within the soul—for basically even religion has become naturalistic now—and bearing them upward into a world of spirit, by developing the capacities for this, we actually encounter Michael... But Michael is a unique being. Michael is a being who in fact reveals nothing unless we bring toward him something from the earth through our own industrious efforts.

Dornach 1924, GA 233a

14 January

There is not just one kind of health but as many kinds of health as there are human beings.

Berlin 1909, GA 57

15 January

It must inevitably lead us deep into the secrets of human existence if we can ask how the human being becomes evil. He does so by using in the wrong place the powers he is endowed with to perfect himself!

Berlin 1914, GA 63

16 January

Only in future will it become possible to fathom many things in the Gospels.

Berlin 1911, GA 124

17 January

Though paradoxical it is true to say that one person, let's imagine a 'statesman'—a word we nowadays usually use ironically—may say all sorts of clever things, things regarded nowadays as clever, but will never have formed a relationship with the supersensible world. What he says, when translated into reality, will bear a germ of death within it. Another, on the other hand, may show no overt sign that he is preoccupied with spiritual science, and unless we know, we may be unaware of this. But he speaks differently about things. What he says, for instance, about social issues, may not betray any sign that he is preoccupied with spiritual science; but the fact that he is gives his ideas a real underlying impulse.

Dornach 1920, GA 196

18 January

True practice of thinking requires us to gain the right attitude, the right feeling about thinking. How can we do so? No one can gain the right feeling for thinking if they believe that it is something that unfolds only within them, in their head alone.

Karlsruhe 1909, GA 108

19 January

Just consider all the things people today wish to draw upon in order to succeed, or be someone—everything except their native spiritual inner life! ... But we have to feel true reality within us, we have to feel our connection with the world of spirit. And we can only do this if everything that connects us with our pre-earthly existence remains intact. And all this is consolidated if a person, as I will put it, has a leaning toward unvarnished truth and truthfulness. Nothing so greatly secures our original, authentic sense of existence as our sense of truth and truthfulness. To feel obliged to test things before we say them, to first seek the parameters within which we can say the things we intend to, helps inwardly consolidate our sense of a worthy human existence.

Dornach 1923, GA 220

20 January

Truly, thought is our most intrinsic quality. If we find the relationship between our thought and the cosmos, the universe, then we also find the connection of our most intrinsic being with this cosmos...There is just one difficulty...most people have no thoughts!...Most of what is called thinking in ordinary life occurs in words. People think in words. This is true to a far greater degree than people generally believe.

Berlin 1914, GA 151

21 January

There is not one, single worldview for the thinker who can penetrate the nature of thinking but 12, equally justified outlooks; they are equally justified in so far as each worldview can be supported by equally valid reasons. There are indeed 12, equally justified outlooks on the world.

Berlin 1914, GA 151

22 January

It is particularly beneficial for people to really practise and experience the various moods of soul—occultism, transcendentalism, mysticism, empiricism, voluntarism, logism, gnosis—so that they can call them to mind, can feel their effect at any moment, as it were, and then place all these moods—as if at one and the same time—into the single constellation of phenomenalism, into the Virgin. Then there will arise before us, with a very distinctive grandeur, something that can disclose the world and its phenomena to us.

Berlin 1914, GA 151

23 January

For anthroposophy, ideas are the vessels, fashioned from love, into which the human being spiritually draws his essence from worlds of spirit.

Stuttgart 1923, GA 257

24 January

Herman Grimm once said that there are four minds, four individuals, to whom the German looks up when, in a sense, he seeks to receive his life's direction. These four figures are Luther, Frederick the Great, Goethe and Bismarck. Grimm says that if German people can no longer look up to the orienting power of these four minds, then they will feel themselves bereft and abandoned within the federation of the world's nations. This comment, which many in the nineteenth century firmly adhered to—though I was not among them—can today weigh rather heavily upon us. We have to acknowledge the following precisely in relation to such a statement: Luther does not essentially and intrinsically live within the traditions of the German character. Goethe, as we have repeatedly said, never came to real life within it; and Frederick the Great and Bismarck belong to a whole fabric that no longer exists. Thus, in these terms, the time would have arrived when the Central European German, the German altogether, would feel himself bereft and abandoned. Nowadays people do not feel things fully enough to really fathom such things within their soul.

Dornach 1919, GA 188

25 January

If you remove the intrinsic and basic strength from human spirituality, that is, freedom, individual freedom, this is exactly like trying to raise someone without giving them anything to eat.

Dornach 1919, GA 188

26 January

I have often had occasion to point out in these reflections that, in relation to the most important life questions, contemporary people can learn from the incisive, profound and indeed overwhelming events of our times; but that only a very few people practise this kind of learning methodically. It is commonly thought that learning from experience is done by judging events then regarding such judgement as experience. This may be very pleasing to people, but is not only entirely inadequate for the needs of our time, for social insights, but also completely inappropriate. What we need to do, instead, is not impose our view upon events but really learn from them—allow events themselves to judge.

Dornach 1919, GA 188

27 January

You see, when people affect our will, when we not only feel strong antipathy or sympathy for them but wish to act out or actively express in some way the sympathy and antipathy we feel, then such people were somehow or other connected with us in a past life. When people make an impression only on our reason or aesthetic sense, they enter our life with no past connection with us from a previous life.

Dornach 1924, GA 234

28 January

Through someone we meet for the first time ever in the universe, we can look more deeply into the world. It is also good fortune to meet someone for the very first time; and we must try to develop a subtle feeling for this fact—that a person we meet for the first time enables us to know the world better. The moment an initiate meets a person with whom he is not karmically connected, whom he meets, we can say, for the first time ever in the cosmos, then he has a duty towards this person: he has the task of connecting with the guardian angel in the sphere of the angeloi who stands by this person with special protectiveness. It is not enough just to become acquainted with the person; we must come to know his guardian spirit too. This person's angel will also in turn speak from our own inwardness with great clarity…This gives the initiate's engagement with the person in question a certain character. He himself adopts something that the angelos seeks to tell this person with whom he becomes acquainted: he transforms into the person's angelos. By this means, what can be said to the person becomes more intimate than is the case for ordinary awareness. It is because of this, too, that the initiate is basically different in character toward each person whom he meets for the first time ever in the universe: in every such instance, he assumes something of the angelos of this person.

Zurich 1924, GA 240

29 January

We must come to feel again that geology does not equate to knowledge of the earth. A huge rocky colossus, surrounded by the surging oceans and by air, is not the earth; and the Milky Way and the stars are not the entirety of the cosmos. The cosmos consists of ahrimanic beings below, and luciferic beings above, who manifest through outward sense phenomena, and beings of the normal hierarchies to whom we raise ourselves when we penetrate both kinds of sense appearance and come to the truth. You see, these beings do not appear intrinsically in outward sense appearance, but only reveal themselves through it.

Dornach 1921, GA 203

30 January

Thus anthroposophy begins everywhere with science, artistically enlivens its ideas, and ends with religious contemplation; it begins with what the head can grasp, then approaches what the Word can configure in its broadest scope, and ends with what the heart imbues with warmth; it leads the heart into certainty so that the human soul can find itself at all times in its true home, in the spirit realm. Upon the path of anthroposophy, therefore, we should learn to start with knowledge, then raise ourselves to art, and end in religious inwardness.

Stuttgart 1923, GA 257

31 January

Two virtues shine their light upon our past incarnations: wisdom, and justice or fairness. Courage and discretion, on the other hand, shine forth upon future incarnations...When people today read *Iphigenia* by Goethe, or Schiller's *William Tell*, they usually think back to their schooldays when they first read these works, and regard them as lying in the past. But that's not right; you see, we should not forget that these works act upon us best when we read them in old age, for then they serve faculties of justice and wisdom.

Zurich 1915, GA 159

February

1 February

The only point of all punishment is to awaken powers in the soul that enable consciousness to engage with circumstances which would otherwise lead to consciousness shutting itself down…and this is also the mission of penitence. Contrition and penitence involve looking at a deed in such a way that its power is raised up into awareness; so that consciousness now surveys the whole context and thus prevents itself being shut down on the next such occasion.

Berlin 1916, GA 166

2 February

Every sentence of the Sermon on the Mount relates to one of the human being's nine members...The Sermon on the Mount should appear transparently before our eyes of spirit as the deed of Christ Jesus through which he entirely internalized what was contained in the old laws of Moses, made it entirely into an inner impulse so that the human I gains agency in the way it must for all of the human being's nine members. You see, when the I takes up and absorbs the Christ impulse, this acts upon all nine members of the human being.

Berlin 1920, GA 116

3 February

The moment we decide to engender within ourselves the thoughts presented by anthroposophic enquiry and research, then we also become able to commit ourselves to its truth with our whole individuality since this enables us to experience the first level of its truth.

Dornach 1923, GA 221

4 February

In the child manifests something that the child cannot presently discern, and which the child, the person, could never perceive even by the time of death if left to their own resources; but this can be perceived in the soul of the other, of the one who in old age looks back upon this child. Here you have something that can reveal itself through the child—not in the child and not in the man or woman into whom this child can develop, and live onward to the moment of death, but in the other who, at a ripe old age, looks lovingly upon the child in earliest life.

Zurich 1919, GA 193

5 February

If we can create more intimate relationships in life between soul and soul, relationships founded on impulses of feeling and will, and if, after a soul has passed through the portal of death, we can primarily hold fast to such feeling-imbued relationships, this interest in the other soul, such curiosity about the answers that it will give; or if we perhaps feel the prompting to signify something for this soul, and can live in these reminiscences that do not derive from the content of our thinking but from soul relationships, then this will fit us particularly to approach the other soul with questions at the moment we fall asleep. By contrast, we are best fitted to receive answers, messages at the moment of awakening, if we have been able and inclined to engage perceptively, discerningly, with the person who has died during their lifetime. Just think how, nowadays especially, people pass each other by in life like ships in the night, without really getting to know one another.

Berlin 1918, GA 181

6 February

In the account of Parzival, if we rightly understand it, we can find all the diverse schoolings of the consciousness soul that are necessary so that this consciousness soul can act in the right way; so that the human being can take possession of the powers that swirl around and contest with each other in the mind or feeling soul. The more that modern human beings go into themselves and try to practise self-knowledge, the more they will find the battle raging within them, a battle within the rational or mind soul.

Berlin 1913, GA 144

7 February

There is no advantage in having no idea whatever about how to keep accounts and ledgers; and it is no blessing for humanity if there are great numbers of people who wish to be idealists who, disdaining to grapple with all kinds of practical matters, seek to surrender themselves to spiritual reflections.

Dornach 1920, GA 196

8 February

Just try to see, to subtly observe, whether a person has dreams in which his outward experiences are strongly, vehemently altered. In such a case you will find you're dealing with a person of strong will; whereas if someone dreams their life more or less as it is, they will be a weak-willed person.

Dornach 1924, GA 234

9 February

Christian yoga is to live your way entirely into the Gospels as if they were your own life of soul. Four things are absolutely necessary for Christian yoga to be at all possible. The first is innocence, simplicity ... we have to recognize that in life we have all kinds of experiences that rob us of our open-mindedness...The second virtue we need to be a Christian mystic is to shed a quality that many people have: the inner sense of wellbeing they gain from religious practices. The third virtue is more difficult. It involves absolutely relinquishing the thought that something is due to our own proficiency. The fourth virtue is to achieve patient surrender to whatever may come to meet us. This preparation will enable a person to progress through the seven stages of the Christian mystic path.

Düsseldorf 1906, GA 97

10 February

Modern human beings should take up what has accrued to them: intellectualism and consciousness of freedom. If we take these up in a fitting way, so that we imbue all other earthly knowledge and all other actions with what flows to us from pure human consciousness, as anthroposophy endeavours, then we will find the powers of Christ in the depths of our soul.

Dornach 1923, GA 221

11 February

The cultivation and especially the self-cultivation of idealism, which cannot be lost as we grow older, is what opens the way to Christ, because it is in turn something acquired in our life between birth and death...This is the will path to Christ. The other path is that of thought. Do not seek abstract ways to Christ nowadays, but instead seek these tangible paths. Contemplate the nature of the path of thought, which means that we become inwardly tolerant for the views of all humanity, that we gain social interest in the thoughts of other people. Contemplate the nature of the path of will and you will not find anything abstract in it but rather the need to cultivate idealism... from this idealism spring the impulses to do more than the sense world prompts us to; springs the aim of acting out of the spirit.

Zurich 1919, GA 193

12 February

Only if we are able to confine ourselves solely to what we have seen can we gradually come to exact thinking.

Dornach 1922, GA 210

13 February

Someone who...seeks gradually to acquire this practical form of thinking, which dwells within things, an objective thinking, must consider three things: firstly, as human beings, if we wish to become practical thinkers, we must have a certain connection with the things and realities around us; and this connection can be expressed as follows: we must try as much as possible to develop interest in the realities and facts of life. Interest in the outer world is the first magical means for acquiring practical thinking. The second is that our own actions and activities must be governed by enjoyment and love. The third is cultivating an inner sense of satisfaction when we think for ourselves, when we go further than life prompts us to, and form our own inward thoughts. These are indeed the three stages, the magical means for all practical thinking: interest in the world around us; enjoyment and love of all we undertake; and inner satisfaction in the reflection, that is, the thinking, that we undertake in our own secluded chamber.

Nuremberg 1909, B 78

14 February

As soon as we dwell within anthroposophy in such a way that the experiences we have there become habitual, this is a very bad thing. Anthroposophy is something that must really be acquired each day anew; there is no other way to possess anthroposophy.

Stuttgart 1923, FA 217a

15 February

Once we own these two insights: of how thoughts weave in the world independently, of living thoughts at work in the world; and of the weaving of thoughts within our own corporeality, then we have a starting point, also founded in feeling, for an inner, meditative work upon our soul so as to ascend now to knowledge of the world of spirit.

Berlin 1917, GA 66

16 February

Nietzsche goes mad because he directly faces the need to enter the supersensible world and is unable to do so. Many other people do not go insane, but I do not wish to elaborate here on why they do not, since even when describing peculiarities of civilization one should adhere still to certain polite bounds of discourse. One thing is apparent in Nietzsche's life: that modern human beings can only be honest toward themselves and others by entering the supersensible world.

Dornach 1923, GA 221

17 February

In the real moral element that inheres in the human individuality, lives in it, the good derives from the interest we have in the other person; that interest we can acquire by feeling what others feel as our own. The origin of immorality, on the other hand, is where people close themselves off, do not develop empathy for others' feelings. Good thinking means, basically, to be able to put ourselves in other people's shoes, while bad thinking means being unable to do so.

Dornach 1923, GA 221

18 February

Human beings must become able again to bear upward to ideas all their soul warmth and soul light. They must again be able to invest their whole being in the spirituality of the world of ideas. This is something we have lost today, really... anthroposophy seeks to point the way to where we do not lose earth-warmth, do not lose earth-light, where we retain our fresh sympathy and interest in all specific details of earthly existence, our love for everything earthly, but at the same time can rise to that lofty realm of ideas where the divine reveals itself in pure concepts. As modern human beings we can no longer feel the divine within us as ancient people on earth did; we first have to ascend to it. This is the mood which allows us to rightly feel the mystery of the Holy Spirit... Through their own strength modern people must re-enliven their concepts, which have grown cold and dead, and then they can reach the Holy Spirit, and by virtue of this can then also see the Mystery of Golgotha in the right light.

Dornach 1923, GA 221

19 February

Now an inner reality will become vividly apparent to all who deepen their study of the New Testament: that life flows directly from the John Gospel, that it bears conviction and a source of truth of a rather different kind from other religious texts. From it flows a certainty that really requires no support from outward facts.

Berlin 1906, GA 94

20 February

Karmic relationships are not of a kind that can be comprehended without more ado. We have to slowly and gradually acquire life's highest insights, the most important insights for illuminating our lives. But people are not keen to hear this or believe it.

Stuttgart 1912, GA 135

21 February

There is ... nothing that militates so greatly against a real conviction about reincarnation and karma as the principle that for the work we do we should be recompensed directly with a wage for this work commensurate with it.

Stuttgart 1912, GA 135

22 February

What is to emerge from anthroposophy must rest upon the sure foundation of human enthusiasm. And this human enthusiasm is something we can only acquire by looking upon the ideal that should live in the breast of every anthroposophist, one great enough to bind members of the Anthroposophical Society together in love. It cannot be denied that in the three phases of anthroposophic development so far the enthusiasm for this ideal—though not the ideal itself—has somewhat faded. And now, as we stand in mourning before the ruins of the building that enabled us to express this ideal in an outwardly manifest language, it is all the more necessary for us to find each other in the right feeling for the anthroposophic ideal so that, out of this shared feeling and the shared thinking that proceeds from it, a strength can arise that we ... greatly need today.

Dornach 1923

23 February

What can be experienced, and is also actually experienced at the moment of falling asleep and that of awakening is particularly important for relationships between people incarnated here in the physical world and the dead… The moment of falling asleep is the most favourable for conveying to the dead all that we have ourselves developed as relationships with particular dead souls. And the moment of awakening is the most favourable for receiving messages from the dead into our physical life on earth… In fact every bereaved person has such relationships, coming to most significant expression at these moments of falling asleep and awakening. But they do not come to awareness because such moments flit by very fast, and people are not used to attending to what approaches their souls in these fleeting moments. Nothing is more helpful for holding fast to what approaches us at such fleeting moments than our preoccupation with the finer, subtler thoughts of spiritual science.

Stuttgart 1918, GA174b

24 February

There is a pupil of Faust, who stands with almost the same importance in humanity's spiritual history as Professor Faust himself—naturally I'm referring to Goethe's *Faust*. And this pupil is none other than Hamlet.

Dornach 1922, GA 210

25 February

What Goethe sought, and what he was unable to achieve, can be seen by reading his *Elective Affinities* (from part two of *Wilhelm Meister*). Goethe sought everywhere to integrate the human being into a greater spiritual context. But he was no longer able to do this, for he had been deprived of Schiller.

Dornach 1922, GA 210

26 February

In the intellectual age... we must rediscover the world of spirit through the intellect, and not by dulling our thinking.

Dornach 1922, GA 210

27 February

We raise ourselves into the supersensible when we experience occurrences in the physical world in a spiritual, idealistic way, so that we learn to feel them as supersensible experiences; when we say: what I have perceived here in the world of the senses comes suddenly to life if I raise it into an ideal. It comes alive if I imbue it in the right way with my sensibility and will impulse.

Stuttgart 1923, GA 257

28 February

We become especially aware of our I when that magical connection with other people or our surroundings occurs, which we call empathy or sympathy. Here we can really see that a magical action passes from soul to soul, from spirit to spirit.

Berlin 1911, GA 124

29 February

When something seemingly destructive, inhibiting and bad exists somewhere, the whole progress of evolution is governed with such wisdom that even this destructive, inhibiting and bad element is transmuted and reconfigured within the whole to produce the good, to turn out for the best.

Berlin 1908, GA 102

March

1 March

The singular thing is that in our fifth post-Atlantean epoch, imaginations have been lost while concepts have been retained for the consciousness soul. Our recent cultural and spiritual life is so prosaic, so arid: everything of a pictorial nature had been squeezed out of it, leaving abstraction, so beloved of those who regard themselves as cultured. Our modern era lives in a sense through abstraction, seeks to reduce everything to some kind of abstract concept. Precisely in what the middle classes call 'practical' life we find abstract concepts widely predominant. But already there are signs—and this is characteristic of our era and will be so especially of the near future—that the depths of the human soul, the subconscious impulses of human souls, are again seeking imaginations; concepts, we can say, that strive toward the quality of imaginations.

Dornach 1919, GA 189

2 March

And in our era, someone who has not otherwise reflected much upon death, who has given little or only partial thought to the world of spirit, can find, after death, a wonderful teacher in death. Specifically in this war, this is something very significant for the connection between the physical world and the world of spirit. I have emphasized this in a few lectures during these grave times: what we can do through mere instruction in words is not sufficient; but huge guidance will come to the people of the future as a result of so many people dying. They [those still living] affect the dead, and the dead, for their part, intervene in the future cultural process of humanity. I can tell you about one such deceased person who recently passed through the gate of death at a young age. I can convey to you words that, if you like, came through to me, words that strike one as surprising to some degree because they testify to how the dead person, who experienced death with special clarity upon the field of battle, now finds his way into this very different mode of experience after death; how he works his way beyond earthly thoughts and into spiritual ones. I would like to share these words with you now. If I can put it like this, these words were discerned, detected, when one who died on the field of battle sought to convey them to those whom he had left behind.

> In luminosity
> I feel
> the power of life.
> Death has wakened me

from sleep,
from spiritual sleep.
I will continue to be
and out of myself
do what the luminous strength
shines out within me.

Berlin 1915, GA 157

3 March

In ordinary waking life people awaken in fact only through the nature of the other person. But the one who has become independent, personal, in the era of the consciousness soul, wishes to awaken through the soul and spirit of the other. He wishes to awaken in relation to the soul and spirit of the other person: he wishes to approach the other in such a way that this other produces in his own soul a shock such as that which outer light and noise and so forth produce upon dream life.

Dornach 1923, GA 257

4 March

In relation to spiritual truths, we must continually develop to the highest degree what can, in the best sense of the word, be called tolerance. Tolerance is needed in the interactions of those who seek to develop anthroposophic spiritual science together.

Dornach 1923, GA 257

5 March

We can say that all of us today die in a way that leaves our thoughts and feelings unprocessed. These thoughts and feelings... remain there, unworked through, and when we have passed through the gate of death, we really all have the urge to continue thinking in the earthly realm, to go on feeling in earthly ways. ... Given this, we can recognize the need today not to lose for earthly life what the dead take unprocessed with them through the gate of death.

Berlin 1918, GA 181

6 March

Just as we undermine our bodily life if we do not sleep in the right way, so we undermine our soul life if we are not rightly awake. We are not awake in the right way if we give ourselves up only to outward impressions, and live without any awareness of our connection with the world of spirit.

Berlin 1913, GA 175

7 March

The path available to human beings that consists of making ever truer the words 'Not I but Christ in me' is a path smoothed for us by the Christ impulse gradually entering our power of memory. As yet this impulse has not come to dwell within it. Once it has done so—when the Christ impulse lives not only in human understanding but when it pours itself through the whole seam, the whole swathe of memory—then people will no longer have to rely, for example, upon learning history from outward documents, for then their power of memory will expand and broaden. Christ will live within this memory. And by virtue of Christ entering their power of memory, and living there, human beings will know that Christ worked from beyond the earth up until the Mystery of Golgotha, preparing it, and then passed through this Mystery of Golgotha; and will know how he continues to work as impulse through history... In future, for us who seek to encompass Christianity in living ways, the following also can hold true:

> In the beginning is memory
> and memory lives on,
> and memory is divine.
> And memory is life
> and this life is the I of the human being
> that streams within the human being himself.
> Not he alone but Christ in him.

When he recalls divine life,
Christ is present in his memory
and as radiant life of memory
the Christ will shine forth
into every immediate and present darkness.

Pforzheim 1914, GA 152

8 March

The interval of the fifth is truly the experience of Imagination. If we truly experience the fifth, we already know subjectively what Imagination is . If we experience sixths, we know what Inspiration is. And if we experience sevenths—if we survive this—we know what Intuition is. What I mean is that the form of the state of soul in the experience of the seventh is the same as that of clairvoyant perception in Intuition. And the state of soul in the experience of the sixth is the same as Inspiration in clairvoyance. Likewise the experience of the fifth is a true imaginative experience. The state of soul in these experiences needs only to be filled with vision. In musical experience such states of soul are certainly present. For this reason you will also often hear that in the ancient mystery schools and in the traditions surviving from them, clairvoyant perception is also referred to as musical knowledge. Everywhere it is pointed out—though people no longer know why—that there is ordinary corporeal knowledge, intellectual knowledge, and spiritual knowledge, the latter really being, though, a musical form of knowledge, a knowledge that lives in the musical element. And basically it would not be so difficult to gain popular affirmation of the teaching of threefold human nature if people were aware of their musical experience and feeling.

Stuttgart 1923, GA 283

9 March

A true process of higher knowledge really only ever involves making conscious what otherwise dwells unconsciously in us during sleep.

Berlin 1915, GA 157

10 March

The only way in which we can develop to higher stages is by leaving behind a lower, positive stage, placing ourselves in a negative mood and in this mood absorbing a new content, and pervading ourselves with this so intensively that we can again become positively active at a higher stage.

Berlin 1910, GA 59

11 March

In sleep it becomes necessary for soul life to let the speech element of earth life resonate in such a way that the angelic world, the world of archangels, can take pleasure in this reverberation of speech life... That which leads speech to picture, to rhythm, to beat, to the melodious and dramatic element, leads it back therefore to soul quality, and within the soul realm raises it through the musical and imaginative element to the world of spirit—we have experienced how this is stripped away and, as I would put it, a further concession has been made to the materialism of language... Language as it is today in all civilized peoples, this language fetters the soul between falling asleep and re-awakening to the merely physical mutterings of the mineral world, to the hum and fizzle of the merely physical content of the vegetable world, and does not give the soul in sleep any conduit to the bright speech of the angeloi, the loud trumpet-speech of the world of archangels with its deep, cosmic meaning.

Dornach 1923, GA 222

12 March

Sleep simply does not receive the right strength, and all that should be drawn from life on earth is simply not drawn, if the right relationship to primordial powers is not invoked by virtue of a person developing those strong inner powers that are necessary if we are to grasp spiritual science.

Dornach 1923, GA 222

13 March

If the cycle of the seasons is once again felt, in a universally human way, as having an inner connection with the Mystery of Golgotha, then this placing of the soul's feeling into the seasons and into the Mystery of Golgotha will at the same time mean that true social feeling becomes widespread across the globe.

Berlin 1917, GA 175

14 March

The following seven stages in Rosicrucian schooling are intended to lead pupils into the world of spirit...

1. What is called 'study' as understood in Rosicrucian circles.
2. What is known as the acquisition of imaginative perception.
3. What is termed acquisition of the occult script.
4. What is either termed, more modestly, as rendering life rhythmic; or also, and authentically, preparation of the philosopher's stone. This is something that does indeed exist and is not that foolish thing that you can read about in some books.
5. What is called knowledge of the microcosm, that is, of one's own human nature.
6. What is termed opening into the macrocosm, or into the great surrounding world.
7. What is known as: attainment of divine blessedness.

Berlin 1907, GA 55

15 March

It is rightly recounted that after the event of Golgotha Christ descended to the dead, into the world of spirit, to bring them the redeeming Word. The Christ event still works today in the same way. Therefore it amounts to the same thing whether a person still lives here in the physical world or whether he has already died: he can still also experience the Christ event in the world of spirit if, while here on earth, he gained understanding of it. Then it will become apparent that a person has not lived here upon our earth without reason. But if someone has gained no understanding for the Christ event here, its effects pass him by without trace in the period between death and a new birth, and he must wait until he returns once more to earth, must wait for rebirth, so that he has the opportunity to prepare himself for this.

Munich 1910, GA 118

16 March

Something different must come to modern people: by unfolding the right powers of their soul experience, they must come to reacquire what once upon a time was lost. I'll put it like this: people must develop a consciousness—after all , we live in the age of the consciousness soul—that what has now become inward must find its way outward again to the divine realm of spirit. And this will for example be possible, as I hinted in response to a question that was asked at the first School course at the Goetheanum, in *one* particular field, if the inner wealth of feelings we can experience in melody passes to the single tone; if people can experience the secret of the single tone and if, in other words, they not only feel the quality of intervals but really also, with inward richness, with inner diversity, they experience the single tone like a melody. Nowadays, as yet, people scarcely have any idea about this.

Dornach 1923, GA 222

17 March

Before the fourth century AD... the spirits of form held sway not only in impressions of the sense world but above all in human thoughts. These thoughts have now passed to the Archai, to the Principalities... certain spirits of form were not able to resolve upon ceding thoughts to the Principalities, the Archai, but kept them for themselves. And thus, amongst the spiritual beings who govern human affairs, we have the rightly evolved powers in possession of the thought world, as well as retrograde spirits of form, retrograde Elohim beings who now still hold sway over the thought world... This means that human beings are exposed to the following: some, whose karma fits them for this, receive the impulses of their thinking from the Archai. This makes their thinking, though it remains objective, their personal possession. They increasingly elaborate their thoughts as their own personal possession. Others, by contrast, do not succeed in elaborating their thoughts as their own personal possession.

Dornach 1923, GA 222

18 March

We have had, let us say, a particular number of earthly incarnations. And if we now have the will—for will is what counts here—then we can find within ourselves the strength to engender our own thought world out of ourselves, as I described in *The Philosophy of Freedom*. But now consider this, and take it most seriously: consider that we are now in the era in which people strive to elaborate and form their thoughts out of their own interiority. But they now also stand there in the world as individuals. These thoughts would in a sense stand there isolated in the world, have no meaning for the cosmos, if beings of spirit did not exist who, in the right way, take the thought a person elaborates in freedom and integrate it into the cosmos, as power and impulse. And thus we have the progress that is given in as much as the governing of thoughts passes from the spirits of form to the spirits of personality.

Dornach 1923, GA 222

19 March

It is not insignificant for the soul if someone tries to understand what has been perceived imaginatively. There are certain remedies that act upon this or that human illness. Today it is already extraordinarily difficult to render medicines effective for people. But if someone has made efforts to understand imaginative pictures with their healthy human understanding, they activate enough of their life force to enable remedies—if they're the right ones—to act more effectively. The organism does not reject them.

Dornach 1922, GA 210

20 March

Someone who is an anthroposophist to their core, in their heart, will discern the character of a foreign city in their blood.

The Hague, GA 145

21 March

When thinking stops during sleep, digestive activity works into consciousness; when the person awakes, if he feels the echo of this within him, this experience can easily become a very accurate barometer, precisely in the developing soul, of healthy or unhealthy nutrition.

The Hague, 1913, GA 145

22 March

The evil which the luciferic spirits brought humankind at the same time as the good deed of freedom will be shed entirely during the course of earthly evolution. The evil which the ahrimanic spirits brought, can be shed as karmic lawfulness unfolds. But the evil which the Asuras bring cannot be remedied in this way. While the good spirits gave the human being pain and suffering, illness and death so that, despite the possibility of evil, he can evolve upwards; and while they gave the possibility of karma to redress error, this will not be so easy to accomplish in relation to the asuric spirits in the course of earth existence. You see, these Asuras will create conditions in which what they encompass and take hold of—which is our deepest inwardness, the consciousness soul and the I—will unite with the earth's sensory nature.

Berlin 1909, GA 107

23 March

It is this that makes it possible for us to change our etheric body in the way that happens in correct esoteric development, which requires also this among other developmental requirements: that we acquire composure, and true understanding of our karma, so that we do not try to use sympathy and antipathy to avoid what must come towards us, or inwardly oppose what happens to us, but instead learn to bear our karma in an even stream of experience. Learning to endure our karma in this way is part of esoteric development, and it is this that makes it possible for us to change our etheric body in such a way that it gradually and increasingly learns to feel the etheric life that outwardly surrounds it.

The Hague 1913, GA 145

24 March

But if someone takes the John Gospel and reads only three lines of it, this is of huge importance for the whole universe. You see, if no earthly soul read the John Gospel, the whole mission of the earth would remain unfulfilled. The spiritual powers that continually infuse the earth with new life, to counter what dies there, flow from our participation in such things.

The Hague 1913, GA 145

25 March

Where do we find our sense of discernment for human beings, our capacity to know human nature? Well, this sense is none other than the one with which we are also endowed for appreciating art—the artistic or aesthetic sense: the sense that can convey to us the shining of the spirit within matter, that manifests to us the beauty we encounter in art. This artistic sense is at the same time what enables us to grasp and perceive a person in their immediate presence and being, in such a way that this perception can also become a direct, living practice.

Stuttgart 1923, GA 304a

26 March

The human being, also in a deeper sense, is far more of a social being than people usually think. And in particular, mental illnesses can very rarely be viewed only in terms, let us say, of an individual biography, an isolated individual. This is almost impossible.

Dornach 1920, GA 314

27 March

Not everything that can be found upon the path of clairvoyance is—and let me put this radically—worthy of reverence; but everything is worth learning about, acquainting oneself with. This is what we must consider. I said that for this present cycle of ours it is especially important to incorporate the results of head clairvoyance into humanity's general spiritual culture; and this really is important.

Dornach 1915, GA 161

28 March

How is it going, really, with your forward progress?

Vienna 1910, GA 119

29 March

There are 12 different images of the individual I. And basically only when we have looked back upon ourselves, from outside our I, from 12 different perspectives, have we comprehended this I of ours in its entirety. This view of the I from without is precisely like the relationship of the 12 constellations of the zodiac to the sun. Just as the sun passes through the 12 signs of the zodiac and possesses a different power within each, just as it appears in one constellation in spring then moves onward and, during the year, passes through each of the 12 signs and thus shines upon the earth from 12 different perspectives, so the human I also illumines itself from 12 different perspectives when it looks back upon itself from the higher world.

Vienna 1910, GA 119

30 March

And here we come to a maxim that should always encourage the spiritual pupil: that everything outwardly physical is only understood if, rather than seeing it on its own terms alone, it is understood as the likeness of a supersensible, a spiritual reality.

Vienna 1910, GA 119

31 March

If someone wishes to intervene in the breathing process, they should do this only with a knowledge that becomes prayerful, filling themselves with deep reverence. Otherwise no instructions in these matters should be given at all, for they require the deepest responsibility. In discernment and knowledge we imbue ourselves with reverence for the grace of those beings whom we approach but to whom we must still look upward since they send their wisdom down to us from the heights of the macrocosm. These are loftier heights than we can encompass with our ordinary knowledge. This arises from spiritual science as a last outcome, fading away like a self-evident prayer:

> May the blessing of God's protecting ray
> fill my growing soul
> so that it can everywhere encompass
> strengthening powers.
> My soul seeks to pledge itself
> to awaken to life within it
> the power of love,
> in this way seeing God's strength
> upon its path of life
> and working as God wills
> with all that it possesses.

Vienna 1910, GA 119

April

1 April

Once we understand how to accompany the cycle of the year in our thoughts, then powers will mingle with our thoughts that once again allow us to hold dialogue with the divine, spiritual forces manifesting from the stars. Human beings have drawn down from the stars the power to establish festivals that possess an inner, human validity. People must establish festivals out of an inner, esoteric capacity.

Dornach 1923, GA 223

2 April

It will have an inspiring effect if people once again shape festivals with the same enthusiasm with which festivals were once inaugurated. This will also have an inspiring effect for our whole spiritual, cultural and social existence. What we need in life will then be present: not abstract spirit on the one hand, and spirit-devoid nature on the other, but spirit-pervaded nature, nature-configuring spirit—for these two are one; and they will once again weave religion, science and art into a single fabric. In harmony with the Michael thought they will grasp the threefold nature of religion, science and art so that these three can be united in the right way in the Easter thought, in creative fashioning of anthroposophic endeavour which can work in religion, art and scientific enquiry and at the same time also differentiate between religious and cognitive discernment. This would then mean, really, that the anthroposophic impulse would involve feeling, at Eastertide, the unity of science, religion and art; and at Michaelmas would mean feeling how these three siblings—who have a single mother, the Easter mother—stand alongside each other but at the same time complement one another. The Michael thought, that should come alive in festive fashion in the cycle of the year, could have an inspiring effect upon all human life.

Dornach 1923, GA 223

3 April

By beginning to feel the whole surrounding world as moral we increasingly become able to acknowledge this etheric or life world behind physical nature.

Helsingfors (Helsinki) 1912, GA 136

4 April

If we sustain these two elements in our mind, our healthy memory that does not conjure illusions before us that we are anything other than what our achievements or efforts reveal, and our conscience, that will not let us regard things as being of less moral consequence than we have hitherto accorded them, but possibly of still more consequence—if we retain these capacities, then our I can never fall asleep when our astral body has awoken. And then we bear the coherence of our I into the world in which we awaken with our astral body, when, as it were, we enter upon waking sleep.

Helsingfors (Helsinki) 1912, GA 136

5 April

What is love? It is something so complex that no one should have the arrogance to define it, to think that they fully understand its intrinsic nature without more ado. We perceive it, but no definition can express it. Yet a likeness, a simple metaphor, will give us one quality of the action of love: a glass of water that, as it is poured out, becomes fuller.

Helsingfors (Helsinki) 1912, GA 136

6 April

If we discern the quest of our time, its deepest, as yet unconscious hopes and longings, we will know that an active urge rests in the depths of souls: the urge for people to find themselves as souls in full activity. The human soul can only be free, with inner assurance and steadiness, if it can develop inner activity. The human soul can only find itself, orient itself, by becoming aware that it is more than it has been passively endowed with by the world; by coming to know itself involved in what it can experience in such activity. And only from the world of spirit can it discern what it is able to take possession of in active ways. As we reflect upon what the science of the spirit gives, our comprehension has to become a collaborative activity; and then spiritual science becomes satisfaction of the deepest subconscious urges in modern souls. Then it meets and answers the most inward and intimate quest of our age.

Vienna 1914, GA 153

7 April

And something more belonged to those festivals also: not only dance, not only music, not only song, but then afterwards listening, hearkening. First the festivals were actively performed, then people were directed to listen to what came back to them. With their dancing, their songs, with all the poetry they had performed, they had sent great questions to the divine, spiritual cosmos. All this had, as it were, streamed upward into the breadths of the cosmos as water streams upward from the earth and forms clouds in the sky, before descending to earth again as rain. In the same way the effects of these human festivals rose upward and now returned again—not as rain of course but as something that revealed itself to human beings as the power of the I. And in those times people had a fine sense for this singular transformation that occurs precisely around the time of St. Johns in the air and warmth mantling the earth.

Dornach 1923, GA 223

8 April

Someone who dies early in life, let us say as the result of an illness; who undergoes a great deal because of such illness, prepares their soul in such a way that their will forces can be strengthened. Dying early or prematurely from an illness strengthens the power of will.

Vienna 1914, GA 153

9 April

Although we place ourselves into shared worlds through our will, the will, in fact, places us into this world as a separate individual, each for ourselves. This shows us specifically how the will constitutes the entirely individual worth of each person, how it is, as it were, our most inward element from this perspective. From this we can see that sense perception and thought are more outward aspects of our interior life, while feeling and will are the deepest element, our interiority per se.

Vienna 1914, GA 153

10 April

Each time we approach an earthly incarnation, we are exposed to the temptation of remaining in the world of spirit; of entering pure spirit and progressing with what we already are, which is now entirely pervaded by the divine, and relinquishing what we could ever more become as human being by pursuing the far-off religious ideal of the divine, spiritual world. The temptation arises to become irreligious for spirit land.

Vienna 1914, GA 153

11 April

Christ is the child of the godhead who recreates awareness of the divinity in the human being.

Vienna 1914, GA 143

12 April

We cannot find Christ with any philosophy, by thinking reflection. This is completely impossible. This is a principle I would advise you to carefully weigh and ponder … to come to Christ it is necessary to augment philosophical truth with the truth of belief; or—since the era of belief is increasingly fading—the other kind of truth that comes from clairvoyant enquiry, which must first develop in the human soul as a free deed.

Vienna 1914, GA 153

13 April

Christ's passage through death at Golgotha is an event through which the first hierarchy reached up into a higher realm. This is why I have always said to you that the Trinity in fact lies above the hierarchies. But it only came to do so in the course of evolution. Evolution occurs everywhere.

Dornach 1923, GA 224

14 April

> We understand the etheric body through Imagination,
> the astral body through Inspiration,
> and the I we understand through Intuition.

...With the most rigorous thinking one can in a sense find things described from the very outset in my book *Theosophy*: physical body, etheric body, astral body, I. And then one can point to how these members of human nature can also be encompassed in perception through Imagination, Inspiration and Intuition.

Dornach 1923, GA 84

15 April

If we become aware of the world-creative powers in the same way we otherwise perceive our memories, then we have the nature of Imagination, and experience the etheric realm of the world. If we become aware, behind speech, of what does not issue outwards from the larynx but from the other side of the universe, that speaks into us from the cosmos but falls silent as it meets the larynx, then we become aware of a further world through Inspiration, a world to which we belong with the third aspect of our human organism, the astral body.

Dornach 1923, GA 84

16 April

Spiritual perceptions do not only have an abstract, theoretical effect but they act as life force, as the soul's lifeblood. Increasingly people will come to recognize that solace and strength and certainty flow from these perceptions and insights.

Stockholm 1912, GA 143

17 April

We can after all formulate a single sentence, point to one single thing, and then, although this is only outwardly characterized, it gives us the starting point for esoteric Christianity, Christian initiation: and this is the death that was experienced in Christ's union with Jesus of Nazareth. The fact of that death, which we call the Mystery of Golgotha, is what needs to be understood out of the principle of Christian initiation.

Stockholm 1912, GA 143

18 April

But increasingly we are moving towards times in which, first of all, mature judgement must be present and then, out of this mature judgement, clairvoyance must develop once more.

Berlin 1914, GA 154

19 April

The Easter festival as Christian festival is one of resurrection. The corresponding pagan festival that falls roughly in the same season of the year is a kind of resurrection festival of nature, a re-emergence of what has, if I can put it like this, naturally slept throughout winter. But here we come to the point where we must emphasize the fact that the Christian Easter festival is in no way one whose inner meaning and reality coincide with the pagan festival of the spring equinox. Conceived as a Christian festival, the Easter festival really looks back to ancient pagan festivals that emerged from the Mysteries and were celebrated in the autumn. The most remarkable thing about the establishment of the Easter festival, whose content very clearly relates to certain ancient Mysteries, is the following: This Easter festival specifically reminds us of the radical, profound misunderstandings that have arisen during the course of human evolution about the most significant matters. What happened during the early Christian centuries was nothing less than a confusion of the Easter festival with a quite different festival, whereby the former was moved from an autumn to a spring festival.

Dornach 1924, GA 233a

20 April

Now there are three virtues that we must consider, on the one hand in relation to the child and on the other also in relation to the whole life of human society. These are three fundamental virtues. The first is what can live in the will to be grateful; the second what can live in the will to love; and the third what can live in the will to duty. Basically these three virtues are the archetypal human virtues. All others are in a sense encompassed by them.

Dornach 1923, GA 306

21 April

Those who seek to enter the world of etheric imaginations have in a sense to reach behind thinking, behind abstract, dead thinking to inwardly living thinking. If one wishes to enter the world of profound silence, that is, into the world where all material-like activity is spiritual and all spiritual life is creative within matter, we not only have to go behind dead thinking to discover living thinking but also go behind audible speech capacity to the inaudible speech capacity underlying it: this is not vocalizing utterance but profound silence, from which, rather than audible words, the Logos speaks out of stillness, precisely through the intensified silence.

Dornach 1923, GA 84

22 April

The true I does not wish to be sought if it is to appear, if it is to reveal itself. In fact it conceals itself when sought. You see, it is found only in love. And love is devotion of one's own being to another being. For this reason the true I must be found as if it were another, a different being.

Dornach 1923, GA 84

23 April

You will find [in the anthroposophic *Calendar of the Soul*] meditations for each week of the year. I'd like to very specially impress these meditative verses upon you for they contain what can be brought to life in the soul and can then really cultivate a living relationship of soul powers with the powers of the macrocosm. What we can call the onward flow of time is governed and guided by spiritual beings who, in their reciprocal interplay, in their living, mutual relationships, really determine time, make temporality, we might say. Now it would be completely abstract and merely allegorical simply to draw a parallel between human experiences of time, the nature of temporality in the human soul, and time as such in the macrocosm. You will find that in reality very different experiences of the human soul—which in some respects have nothing to do with time at all—are involved here. If you bring these things to life within you, you will come to know the relationship that the soul can experience between its centre and the periphery of sense experiences. This singular relationship can be changed by means of these meditations. Through them, an imagination can be invoked of the relationship between beings who determine the onward progress of time; through these 52 verses, one can find a way from the microcosm to the macrocosm.

Berlin 1912, GA 133.

24 April

In 1911 Franz Brentano wrote a really wonderful book about Aristotle in which he elaborated on the ideas and concepts he wished to particularly impress upon the contemporary world. This is a remarkable karma of our era that Franz Brentano wrote a comprehensive book precisely on Aristotle, which everyone should read if they wish to engage with a certain kind of thinking. This book by Brentano is also very readable... And here, in connection with Aristotle, there is something that must be said to contemporary people when they raise the following question: How can they find a sure path to open within themselves the sources of the Mystery of Golgotha; how can they safely pass through the inner soul experiences that arise when, in their meditative life, as described in our texts such as *Knowledge of Higher Worlds*, they concern themselves with these riddles? You see, we can say that Aristotle seeks to enliven in himself the kind of inner experience that those who ask such a question would need to imitate and similarly evoke.

Berlin 1917, GA 175

25 April

Basically, all our spiritual science is a search for the lost Word.

Berlin 1916, GA 167

26 April

Sometimes, in one or another domain of life, something occurs which the people who see it very understandably only castigate, regarding it only as ghastly, horrible. Nevertheless, the ghastly and horrible possesses something that people find extraordinarily fascinating, that roots them to the spot. This will increasingly be the case.

Dornach 1924, GA 236

27 April

If you go about… with a sensory apprehension healed by outer architectural forms that are now truly constructed out of what is human, then you gain a feeling which more ancient people had for the blows of fate. If you develop what lies between these two, between a feeling for what is truly architectural and a feeling for the truly symbolic quality that passes inwards, then you find a receptivity for blows of fate. You will then feel that things that happen originate in former lives on earth… And amongst everything else that has been accentuated, this Goetheanum, this Goetheanum building with the whole manner in which anthroposophy would have been practised within it, educated people in karmic vision. This education in karmic perception needs to enter modern civilization.

Dornach 1924, GA 236

28 April

It is the I that raises the human being; it is the astral body that works into our sense of speech within our upright being; it is the etheric body that penetrates all this with the power of thinking... how we come close to the angeloi depends a great deal upon how thinking shapes itself during waking life. Whether or not we approach the archangeloi in worthy fashion depends on whether we use our powers of speech worthily. And the way in which we rightly use our capacity of movement and our moral sense determines whether we can approach the archai in worthy fashion.

Prague 1923, GA 224

29 April

A new era must come when human beings, through their own will, must inaugurate a realm in which they can re-enliven dead thinking by their own power. This was a prophecy from the time of the Mystery of Golgotha. Outwardly also this realm did approach. Only people of the modern era can comprehend and assimilate it. Now we must feel that the realm of God, of which Christ speaks, must be seen by us on earth inasmuch as Christ works upon the earth.

Prague 1923, GA 224

30 April

The child is a corporeal-religious being. It is actually true to say that the child is surrendered with his body to the outer physical world and its moral content in the same way that, in a religious mood, we can be surrendered to something that reveals itself to us as divine.

Prague 1923, GA 84

May

1 May

Since we do not invoke a process of destruction in our nervous system when we think meditatively, such meditative thinking never makes us sleepy however long we continue it, whereas our ordinary thinking can do so.

London 1913, GA 152

2 May

He, Michael, is the pre-eminent and most important being in the hierarchy of the archangels... Just as, in ancient Hebrew times—which directly prepared the Mystery of Golgotha—the ancient Hebrew initiates could turn to Michael as the outer manifestation of Yahve or Jehovah, so now we are able to turn toward Michael. He has changed from being the messenger of Jehovah to that of Christ, and during the next few centuries will increasingly receive spiritual revelation from him, which will unveil the Mystery of Golgotha to us more and more.

London 1913, GA 152

3 May

Nothing will help us more to inform abstract ideals with a personal character than to permeate our whole life of spirit with the Christ impulse.

Munich 1911, GA 127

4 May

And so, to discover karmic connection, it is also important when we encounter someone in life, not to consider only what we experience having met him, but also to recognize—for this can be illuminating—that what we experienced in our subtlest inner soul beforehand, which only subsequently lights up in us, is connected with what we then saw in this person or perceived of him or through him.

Dornach 1924, GA 236

5 May

Everyone is clairvoyant, but people deny this theoretically even though they cannot deny it in practice. If they could deny this in practice, it would destroy all life.

Munich 1918, GA 271

6 May

Firstly, a central experience. One cannot be a spiritual investigator from morning to evening. Beholding the world of spirit is linked to certain times: one knows the beginning and end of the state in which the soul penetrates the spiritual world. In this condition, by its own power, the soul is able to divert its attention fully away from outward sense impressions, leaving nothing of outward colours, tones and so forth. It is precisely through this beholding of nothing that perception of the world of spirit arises.

Munich 1918, GA 271

7 May

The Mystery of Golgotha took place on a Friday: on 3 April of the year 33, at three o'clock in the afternoon.

Cologne 1912, GA 143

8 May

As regards love and compassion, we could really speak of a 'programme'—to put it bluntly—that spiritual science should fulfil in future.

Cologne 1912, GA 143

9 May

If one tries to rush on from one new thing to the next, one does not gain the inner constancy to pursue what germinates and bears fruit in the soul; you see, it is really a matter, instead, of letting things mature within us. To do so we have to entirely shed a habit that is in many respects very common today. We have to accustom ourselves to active inner work, a working in the spirit. And this is what helps to bring about things such as those I have described today—to prepare the inner state of soul essential, after the third day, for perceiving the karmic aspects of any occurrence. And altogether this is the way to proceed if you wish to discern spiritual things. You have to say to yourself from the outset that only a beginning is made, and nothing more, when you turn your thoughts in some way to a spiritual context; and that if you want to have an immediate result, this is quite impossible. You have to be able to wait.

Dornach 1924, GA 236

10 May

Observing the surrounding world, the prepared soul can exclaim, 'This is you!' For the soul of Christian Morgenstern, the wisdom of 'This is you!' streamed forth from the Gospel of John.

Cassel 1914, GA 261

11 May

Yes, I have to say when I look back at my Mystery Plays that the figure of Strader is extinguished for me most of all by the living impressions of this archetype of my Strader figure in its life after death. This is scarcely so at all for the other figures.

Dornach 1924, GA 236

12 May

As long as someone dwells on earth he has to ensure, and others also have to ensure, that he remains on the earth as long as possible and that he can be as healthy as at all possible.

Berlin 1914, GA 154

13 May

The time will come when human beings can again have experiences in the supersensible world. And then they will no longer need religion.

Berlin 1908, GA 102

14 May

All wonder and astonishment that has come to expression in us on earth since the fourth post-Atlantean cultural epoch in the phase of human evolution that began with the Mystery of Golgotha, all wonder and astonishment that can live in us, eventually arrives with Christ and helps form the astral body of the Christ impulse. And all love and compassion that occupies human souls forms the etheric body of the Christ impulse. And the conscience that lives in human beings and animates them, from the Mystery of Golgotha to the end goal of the earth, forms the physical body, or what corresponds to it, for the Christ impulse.

Berlin 1912, GA 133

15 May

But we in Central Europe are called upon to have the roses upon the cross; to have what can only be expressed by the connection of the roses with the cross, the roses upon the cross. And in gazing at the rigid cross, we feel that what has entered the world as dead and rigid matter has come into the world from the divine. It is as if spirituality has created for itself a sphere in the material world: *Ex deo nascimur*. We feel also that, if we rightly understand it, we may not only enter the world of spirit with Lucifer but that we die by uniting ourselves with what has descended from the higher, divine Self into the world: *In Christo morimur*. And in the union of the cross with the roses, of material outlooks with the spiritual outlook, we feel how the human soul can awaken in the spirit: *Per spiritum sanctum reviviscimus*. For this reason the cross wound round with roses became the symbol of someone who, in Central European culture, had a deep affinity with spirituality—Goethe. And for this reason it must be our symbol.

Prague 1915, GA 159

16 May

This is the important transition from olden times to the modern era: in ancient India, the pupil needed to practise passive surrender as far as possible; later this was also true still for Augustine and Francis of Assisi. All these humble people allowed themselves to be inspired by what lived in them, what was woven into them. But now the I should bear questions within itself. Every soul today who simply passively accepts what is given it will not get beyond itself, and can then only observe what occurs around it in the physical world. The soul has to ask questions nowadays, must raise itself above itself, grow beyond itself. The soul has to ask as Parzival had to ask about the secrets of the Grail castle. Today, therefore, spiritual enquiry begins with questioning. Souls in whom spiritual science kindles questions, who ask and seek, are Parzival souls.

Kristiania (Oslo) 1909, GA 109

17 May

If you seek ways to communicate with the dead you may even find the means to communicate with them in earthly words, to ask them questions and to receive replies.

Kristiania (Oslo) 1923, GA 226

18 May

The spiritual-scientific outlook must become so alive that the chasm dividing the so-called dead from the living is overcome; so that we feel the dead as souls living amongst us. It is not mere theory we want, but life.

Linz 1915, GA 159

19 May

The Gospel of John is an initiation book about methods of initiation while the Apocalypse concerns the content of initiation.

Munich 1907, GA 284

20 May

No being can fully love another if this love is not a free gift toward the other. My hand does not love my organism. Only a being who is independent, not bound to the other being, can love the other. For this, the human being had to become an I being. The I had to be implanted into threefold human corporeality in order for the earth to fulfil its mission of love through humankind.

Hamburg 1908, GA 103

21 May

J—B. The red pillar is designated J, the purple one B.

The verses on the pillars will bring to mind what is connected with these separate pillars. On the red pillar are the words:

> In pure thought you will find
> the self that can sustain itself.
> When you transform the thought into image
> you will experience creating wisdom.

If you meditate on this, the power of your thought will infuse your red blood pillar with the strength that leads to the goal: to the pillar of wisdom.

The life pillar is infused with the strength it needs if you surrender to the thought that stands upon the other pillar, the blue one:

> Condensing feeling into light,
> you reveal formative power.
> Reifying will into living being,
> you create in world existence.

The first words are concerned with perception and knowledge, the second with life. The formative power 'reveals' itself first of all, in the sense of the first verse; it becomes 'magical' only in the sense of the second verse. To ascend from the mere power of knowledge to magical action or effect lies in the transition from the power of the verse on the first pillar to that of the verse on the second.

Munich 1907, GA 284

22 May

There is no spiritual knowledge that could not flow into active working life.

Munich 1907, GA 99

23 May

More important that all other social reflections and suchlike—which can only lead to anything in our current confused circumstances if they encompass the spirit—would be for a group of insightful people to form, and together establish out of the cosmos again something like a Michaelmas festival on earth; one worthy of the Easter festival, but its autumn counterpart.

Berlin 1923, GA 224

24 May

At the end of the eighties, when I spoke at Vienna's Goethe Association on 'Goethe as the Father of a New Aesthetic', there was a very scholarly Cistercian in the audience. I was describing Goethe's idea of art; and Father Wilhelm Neumann, a Cistercian who was at the same time professor in the Faculty of Theology at Vienna University, said this curious and remarkable thing: The seeds of this lecture you have given today can already be found in Thomas Aquinas!

Dornach 1920, GA 74

25 May

We hear the name of the Logos, and we hear it call out to Moses in those times, 'I am the I AM'. Here the Logos utters its name; it utters what we can initially understand of it through our reason, through the intellect. And what is uttered there appears in the flesh as the incarnated Logos in Christ Jesus.

Hamburg 1908, GA 103

26 May

Under the ashes, as it were, the truth goes on glimmering. It can be covered over by prejudices and impotence, and yet it goes on working secretly as the self-discipline, self-cultivation of thought. And one who believes he must represent spiritual science has to hope that this spiritual-scientific self-cultivation of thinking will smooth the way. He must find his way to the most rigorous logic of Hegel, and only thus can he find a firm foundation in thought for what he must draw down from higher spiritual worlds in forms that are often light and loose as thistle-down. You see, in the realm of the supersensible there is nothing, if we can put it like this, that a rigorously cultivated thinking need reject. A sharper, self-cultivated, disciplined thinking will find the bridge that leads us from the ultimate and highest offspring of the physical plane—thinking—into the supersensible.

Hamburg 1910, GA 120

27 May

All matter on earth is condensed light! ... Every stirring of the soul, wherever it appears, is in some way or other modified love ... Love and light are the two elements, the two components that pervade all earthly existence: love as earth existence of soul nature, light as outward, material earth existence... All earthly conditions are in some way states of equilibrium between light and love. And any disruption or disorder of the equilibrium between light and love is unhealthy.

Hamburg 1910, GA 120

28 May

If we are gradually to possess the other half of evolution, overcoming Lucifer and Ahriman again, then we must permeate ourselves with wisdom and love. As we develop wisdom and love, we develop the elements that will again flow forth from our souls themselves as gifts for those luciferic and ahrimanic powers that sacrificed themselves in the first half of evolution to give us what we need to attain our freedom. We will need to give these powers what we evolve in this way as wisdom and love.

Hamburg 1910, GA 120

29 May

No one could think abstract thoughts, really have thoughts and ideas, if they were not clairvoyant. The pearl of clairvoyance is embedded in our ordinary thoughts and ideas, you see, from the very beginning. These thoughts and ideas arise precisely through the same process of soul through which the highest powers arise. And it is enormously important to learn to understand, first of all, that the beginning of clairvoyance is really something very mundane and everyday: we need only grasp the supersensible nature of concepts and ideas. We have to realize that concepts and ideas come to us from supersensible worlds—only then do we see things rightly... Something a great Enlightenment figure of the eighteenth century said was regarded as hugely important. He said this: O man, dare to use your power of reason. Today we must take to heart a saying of still greater importance: O man, dare to regard your concepts and ideas as the beginnings of your clairvoyant powers.

Helsingfors (Helsinki) 1913, GA 146

30 May

Nothing better guides and governs our moral impulses, in fact, than taking real interest in things and beings.

Norrköping 1912, GA 155

31 May

If people allow what is recorded and recounted in the John Gospel to work upon them sufficiently, then their astral body will be on the way to becoming a 'Virgin Sophia', will become receptive to the 'Holy Spirit'.

Hamburg 1908, GA 103

June

1 June

As we sunder logical thinking from the organism with which it is really bound up, we delve with this thinking into the outward rhythm of the world; indeed, it is only now that we experience that such an outward rhythm exists. As the yogi once brought the inner rhythm of his body to awareness, an outward world rhythm dawns on our awareness in a spiritual way. If I can put this metaphorically: in our ordinary mind we connect thoughts logically, thus using thinking as a means to know the outer sense world. But now we let thinking run into a kind of musical element, which is, though, very much an element of knowledge; we perceive a rhythm that exists upon the ground of all things as a spiritual rhythm; we penetrate into the world as we begin to perceive in the spirit. From being an abstract, dead thinking, a mere thinking in pictures, our thinking becomes inwardly enlivened.

Vienna 1922, GA 83

2 June

Within earth evolution there is no single being who was able to give as much to the single human soul as Krishna.

Helsingfors (Helsinki) 1913

3 June

The same Jesus boy of whom the Luke Gospel tells is initially the incarnation of this same soul who had never previously lived in a human body; and yet is still a human soul due to having been so during the ancient Lemurian era in which our real evolution began. It is the same soul that manifested as Krishna.

Helsingfors (Helsinki) 1913, GA 146

4 June

In the world of spirit there is a very particular law whose whole meaning we can try to clarify with an example. Let us imagine that in a certain year some properly schooled clairvoyant perceived a particular thing in the world of spirit. Now imagine that ten or twenty years later another, equally schooled clairvoyant perceives the same thing, even if he knows nothing of the findings of the first. If you were to believe this, though, you would be sorely mistaken, for in fact a reality of the world of spirit which has once been discovered by a clairvoyant or an occult school, cannot be investigated a second time if the second investigator has not first been informed that it has already been investigated. Thus if a clairvoyant investigated something in 1900, and in 1950 another has come to the point of being able to perceive the same thing, he can only do so if he has previously learned and discovered that someone else has already discovered and investigated it. Realities in the spiritual world that are already known can therefore only be beheld if one decides to learn of them and come to know them in ordinary ways. This is the underlying law that establishes everlasting universal fraternity in the spiritual world.

Budapest 1909, GA 109

5 June

Let us think for a moment about daily life. Picture someone who rushes around, encountering many different things that he could reflect upon, that he could assimilate in spirit; but he makes no effort whatsoever to transform what he experiences, to work upon it, or even to reflect upon it more deeply. He wishes only to 'experience' things, and rushes from one sensation to the next. Then there is another kind of person who passes through life without concerning himself in the least with the outer world. Such people are wrapped up in their own thoughts and fail to notice what is going on around them. Neither of these extremes do a person any good. But there is a middle way: to weave one's own thoughts through everything one experiences. This middle condition is the most wholesome for people in their outer lives.

Copenhagen 1910, GA 125

6 June

To study in the Rosicrucian sense is to be able to immerse oneself in a content of thought that is taken not from physical reality but from the higher worlds. This is what is known as living in pure thoughts... Someone who seeks to delve upward into higher worlds must accustom themselves to the kind of thinking in which one thought is allowed to proceed from the last. Such thinking is elaborated in my books *The Philosophy of Freedom* and *Truth and Science*.

Munich 1907, GA 99

7 June

Being at home nowhere is after all basically—or it can be—a detour whereby, after achieving this sacred place of dislocation, we find the way back again to the substance of nationhood, find harmony again with native qualities in humanity's evolution. While I must draw attention to this at the very outset, on the other hand, in our era in particular, there are good reasons for very open-minded, unprejudiced discussion of the mission of the different folk souls.

Kristiania (Oslo) 1910, GA 121

8 June

But this is what must be observed in all ... peoples: that a singular collaboration arises in them between these three powers—between the normal folk spirit or archangel, the atypical or abnormal archangel, and between what is inwardly at work in the abnormal spirit of the time, who works from within outwards rather as *zeitgeist*, and what, finally, the true *zeitgeist* has inwardly endowed a particular nation with. To truly know and understand a nation, a people, we must inwardly attend to these powers, examining the share that each of these factors has in the national constitution.

Kristiania (Oslo) 1910, GA 121

9 June

If there is a possibility to incarnate, if there is a people, a nation, in the upward trajectory of its life, in upward-striving, flourishing strength, then the archangel descends in the same way that a human being descends after passing through the life between death and a new birth. The archangel descends similarly into a people and incarnates within it. In the same way the archangel experiences his death, the need to withdraw again from the nation in question when the various perceptions, the centres he perceives, start being less actively productive, when they begin to have less content. Then the time arrives when he departs from the community of a nation; then he enters his devachan, his life between death and new birth, later once again seeking out a nation when the opportunity arises in a different way.

Kristiania (Oslo) 1910, GA 121

10 June

Humanity had to go westwards to die as a race. To refresh humanity with new, rejuvenated strength, the move eastwards occurred—from Atlantis across Europe to Asia. Then a move westwards is repeated once again.

Kristiania (Oslo) 1910, GA 121

11 June

What is the real mission of the earth therefore? If you connect the endowment of will with the mission of Saturn, the endowment of feeling primarily with the mission of Sun evolution, and the endowment of the thought element primarily with the mission of Moon evolution—that is, what is contained in the human astral body—then the mission we must connect with the Earth stage is that of establishing complete balance of these three elements, each of which had the upper hand in one of the three preceding planetary stages. Thus these three elements, no longer predominant as each was in one of the earth's previous incarnations, should attain a state of balanced interplay. That is the mission of our earth... The mystery of this mission is expressed in these terms: that through this interplay, this harmonious balance of the three powers, inner life does indeed bring about something productively new. A fourth element is engendered to complement the three preceding ones, and this fourth element is the *element of love*.

Kristiania (Oslo) 1910, GA 121

12 June

In the way it arose and developed out of the potentiality of the archangel, the pictures of Germanic [Nordic] mythology most significantly resemble the worldview that is gradually to develop for humanity as spiritual science. It will be a matter of the kind of development possible for the predispositions which an archangel once introduced into the world—how they can develop once this archangel has benefited from his education through the Christ *zeitgeist*.

Kristiania (Oslo) 1910, GA 121

13 June

There are seven secrets of life which have hitherto never been uttered outside of the occult fraternities. Only in our present era is it possible to speak of them exoterically. They are also called the seven inexpressible or nameless secrets… The secrets are these:

> First: The secret of the abyss.
> Second: The secret of number. This can be studied in Pythagorean philosophy.
> Third: The secret of alchemy. This can be grasped through the works of Paracelsus and Jakob Boehme.
> Fourth: The secret of [birth and] death.
> Fifth: The secret of evil, which is touched upon in the Apocalypse.
> Sixth: The secret of the Word, of the Logos
> Seventh: The secret of blessedness; this is the most deeply hidden secret.

Paris 1906, GA 94

14 June

This is the great mission of Theosophy: to strengthen the faith of human beings again, to make them happy in love and constant in hope.

Vienna 1911, GA 127

15 June

At the heights of the culture of the sixth post-Atlantean cultural epoch... the human being will feel every person's suffering as his own... Everyone will regard complete freedom of religious thought as a necessarily human trait. And the third thing will be this: that people in the sixth cultural epoch will only regard spiritual insights and knowledge as knowledge at all... It will be quite self-evident then that science only holds true if... it is founded on spiritual discernment.

Düsseldorf 1915, GA 159

16 June

By virtue of the fact... that these outward movements have no purpose as such, the gestures thus drawn forth from the etheric body manifest in eurythmy. The human being becomes inwardly free to a large extent. His soul is bodied forth into outer visibility.

Dornach 1923, GA 277

17 June

In Christian esotericism, creating out of relationships is called creating in the spirit. And creating out of true, beautiful and virtuous relationships is called the Holy Spirit in Christian esotericism. The Holy Spirit inspires us when we are able to create what is right, true, beautiful and good out of nothing... Christian esotericism is connected with the deepest thought we can possibly have about all evolution: the thought of creation out of nothing.

Berlin 1909, GA 107

18 June

This has always been the first step in initiation: to have a person during daily life do something that resonates on into sleep life. Everything referred to as meditation, concentration and the other practices a person has undertaken during daily life are nothing other than inner, soul exercises whose effects do not die away when the astral body departs, but instead resonate onward and become formative powers in the astral body at night. This is known as the cleansing of the astral body, a cleansing of what is not appropriate to the astral body. This was the first step, also known as catharsis, or cleansing.

Nuremberg 1908, GA 104

19 June

Only by engaging a little more precisely with the nature of initiation can we gradually come to understand this significant religious testament of the Apocalypse.

Nuremberg 1908, GA 104

20 June

Through Jakim we enter earthly life, assuredly through Jakim: what is outside in the macrocosm now lives within you, you are now a microcosm, for the word 'Jakim' means the divine poured out upon the world within you. Boas, the other pillar means: the entry into the world of spirit through death. We can roughly summarize the word Boas as meaning: What I have hitherto sought within me, the strength, I will find it poured out over the whole world, and within that will I live… Each of these pillars is a one-sided embodiment of life, for life exists only in the balance between them. Neither Jakim nor Boas are life on their own; the first is the transition from the spirit to the body, and the second is the transition from the body to spirit. The thing that matters is the balance between them.

Berlin 1916, GA 169

21 June

Having anthroposophy as theory... is no great accomplishment. It has to come to life. And in particular it can come to life in us by rendering our souls energetic, resilient, courageous; so that at the moment we are anxious about physical life on earth, and wrapped in the profoundest grief and deepest misery, we can be filled by inner joy, inner solace, inner energy as we look up to a world of spirit. Then anthroposophy will be for us like a living being, one who walks amongst us. And only then has it become for us what it should be, only then does it imbue all our activity.

Stuttgart 1923, GA 224

22 June

Karma already lies in what we see of the world, assigned us by the world of the hierarchies.

Dornach 1924, GA 236

23 June

For someone like the author of the John Gospel, everything he knew, everything he could encompass in clairvoyant vision, summoned him to understand the greatest event of earth evolution. Of all that he could learn through clairvoyant perception he said, I must use it to understand the figure of Christ and his mission. Underlying the efforts of the one who wrote the Apocalypse was the prompting to use all esoteric knowledge to explain this event of Golgotha. What he could learn in esoteric science he regarded in no other way than as a wisdom that could serve to understand this event, which he placed in such magnificence before our souls that we can gradually see what it came to mean for him.

Nuremberg 1908, GA 104

24 June

The Rosicrucians are a community that from the fourteenth century onwards cultivated a spiritual, a truly spiritual Christianity within European culture. This Rosicrucian community which, apart from all outward historical forms, sought to reveal the deepest truth of Christianity to its adherents, always also called the latter 'John Christians' ... And what was also the most essential and important thing especially for the John Christians of Rosicrucian communities was the fact that in every human soul lives something that has a direct connection, a relationship, to what took place in Palestine through Christ Jesus. If Christ Jesus can be called the greatest event for humanity, then what corresponds to the Christ event within the human soul must also be the greatest and most significant thing for it. What can this be? Rosicrucian pupils answered this question by saying: for every human soul there is something that can be termed 'awakening' or 'rebirth' or 'initiation'.

Cassel 1909, GA 112

25 June

At that moment so vividly described by the author of the John Gospel when he says that the spirit descended in the form of a dove and united with Jesus of Nazareth, we have the birth of Christ—the Christ is born in the soul of Jesus of Nazareth as a new, higher I. Until that moment another I, that of a great initiate, had developed to the point where it was ripe for this occurrence.

Cassel 1909, GA 112

26 June

It is a cosmic law that if any higher condition is to arise, what previously existed must first be repeated.

Cassel 1909, GA 112

27 June

Human beings develop feelings that transform into love, and in offering such feelings to their fellows, at the same time they enliven those around them. We need only picture to ourselves the enlivening effect that love can have upon those receiving it; how those who are really able to pour out love upon fellow human beings can enliven, comfort and elevate them through this love alone. Here we see that a person has the gift of offering something up. But however much we acquire this capacity for sacrifice, it is as little compared to that of the Thrones. Yet evolution involves beings increasingly acquiring the capacity to offer sacrifice, ultimately even of their own substance and essence, feeling it as the greatest bliss to offer up the substance they have themselves evolved.

Cassel 1909, GA 112

28 June

Lucifer endowed the human being with freedom and independence; Christ transformed this freedom into love. And by uniting with Christ, human beings are led to spiritual love.

Cassel 1909, GA 112

29 June

Christ is so great that every new epoch must discover new means to discern him. In previous centuries, other modes and forms of striving for wisdom were needed. Today, anthroposophy is needed. What we possess today in anthroposophy for understanding Christ will continue to hold good for long eras. You see, anthroposophy will show itself to be something that kindles all human capacities of knowledge. Human beings will gradually grow into an understanding of Christ. But even the anthroposophic view is only, initially, a transitional one. We are aware of this, and also aware that something great, yet couched in transient thoughts, will still need to be framed in greater thoughts.

Cassel 1909, GA 112

30 June

Through the spirit that streamed out as the Christ impulse, something streams into the body that can otherwise only be elicited by means of physical and physiological evolution: through fire, inner fire that expresses itself in blood circulation. John the Baptist still immersed people, at which their etheric body was lifted out so that they saw the world of spirit. But if we allow the Christ impulse to act, it works so that the experiences of the astral body pour into the etheric body and the human being becomes clairvoyant. This can explain the expression 'baptizing with the spirit and with fire'. And this can also bring home to you the real difference between the baptism of John and that of Christ. Through the Christ impulse, a new order of initiates became possible.

Cassel 1909, GA 112

July

1 July

What characterizes the death on the cross for this Christ being? We have to say that it is an event that makes no distinction between the preceding life and the life that follows. This is the essential thing about the death of Christ—that he remains the same; that he was One who embodies the meaninglessness of death. And so those who knew the nature of Christ's death always held to the living Christ.

Cassel 1909, GA 112

2 July

Only someone who can read, and who knows what matters here, can sense the great, the mighty meaning of the John Gospel. The mission of theosophy today is to set this great meaning before the soul. But there is still more contained in this John Gospel. Our observations on the John Gospel will be succeeded by other expositions containing a greater wisdom than ours. And their wisdom will serve to uncover new truths, in the same way that our wisdom has for the past 30 years served to uncover things that cannot be found without theosophy.

Cassel 1909, GA 112

3 July

I beg you to be clear from the outset that it is inevitably difficult to comprehend what actually occurred at the baptism by John, for it was the greatest event of earthly evolution.

Cassel 1909, GA 112

4 July

If you were to investigate the blood of modern human beings—not by chemical means but by those that are available to spiritual enquiry—as well as that of people a few millennia before the appearance of Christ, you would find that this blood has changed; that it has assumed a character that renders it ever less a bearer of love.

Cassel 1909, GA 112

5 July

Thus an impulse had to come to the earth to renew the ancient store of wisdom that had been used up, to implant new life in the etheric body; so that the physical otherwise destined to decay can attract to itself the imperishable, can fill itself with an etheric body that renders it imperishable and redeems it from the downward course of earth evolution. This life introduced into the etheric body was what Christ brought. The fact that what otherwise would have been wedded to death, the human physical body, will be transformed, will be preserved from corruption, is connected with Christ; with the fact that it receives the capacity to attract to itself what is imperishable. The Christ impulse poured life into the human etheric body—new life after life had been consumed! And when we look into the future, we must say this: when my etheric body eventually detaches itself fully from the physical body, I must by then have evolved to the point where the etheric body is entirely pervaded by Christ. Christ must live within me. In the course of my earthly evolution I must gradually completely imbue my etheric body with Christ.

Cassel 1909, GA 112

6 July

If the human being had always known that death is the seed of life, he would not have come to his self-reliant, independent I-hood but would have remained united with the world of spirit. But in this way death arrived, giving him the illusion that he was sundered from the spiritual world, and thus brought up the human being to become an independent I.

Cassel 1909, GA 112

7 July

The miracle of the Resurrection is something only conceivable for those whose thinking is no longer reliant on the instrument of the physical brain.

Cassel 1909, GA 112

8 July

In ordinary gestures in which, alongside uttered words, we express what we wish to say, beings of an angelic-like nature help us to enlarge our earthly speech. But if such ordinary gestures are transformed into the articulate gestures of eurythmy, then, if we conceive these visible forms as changed into a speech that flows from being to being, this is really what the archangels speak to one another.

Dornach 1923, GA 277

9 July

I have often pointed out that in future we can again expect a time—and this will be particularly apparent in the third millennium—when no one will be able to exist without a certain retrospective gaze to former lives on earth, and especially without a clear consciousness that they can have future lives on earth. But this consciousness will appear differently in different regions of the globe, and it is extraordinarily important to understand this.

Berlin 1918, GA 181

10 July

It strengthens us if we encompass life lovingly, rather than unimaginatively rejecting connections whose meaning lies in nothing other than bringing together things seemingly widely divergent. Try doing this in the most ordinary, everyday contexts—you will find that every moment brings opportunities for this; try to allow whatever you experience to ramify into unseen connections. Of course we shouldn't become fantasists, which we can do if we seek more in these mysterious interconnections than they actually are as a vehicle for real perception. But in fact it is not a matter of perceiving something else through such connections but rather of letting them resonate within us. In this way we can live our way slowly into a power that, currently at work in us as thinking, corresponds to the reality of our subsequent incarnation.

Berlin 1917, GA 176

11 July

Truly it is necessary, especially if we delve into the depths of spiritual science, to keep humour alive in us—not continually to feel obliged to wear the long face of tragedy.

Berlin 1916, GA 169

12 July

To feel as if the human being extends far beyond what the soul can achieve with the strength it has so far acquired in its past evolution on earth—this is the right preparatory, Christian mood. And when the soul then finds what it must necessarily know to be bound up with its intrinsic being, but for which it does not find the strength within itself—if the soul then finds what gives it these powers, then what it has found is Christ.

Norrköping 1914, GA 155

13 July

Through what occurs at Golgotha, something that previously could only be attained in spiritual heights unites with earthly humanity itself. Since Christ passed through death on Golgotha, this lives within all human souls. It is the power by virtue of which every soul can find the path into the world of spirit.

Norrköping 1914, GA 155

14 July

Christ-imbued idealism contains the seed of reality. Those who really understand Christ regard ideals as something which do not as yet contain an intrinsic pledge of their reality in the way a plant seed contains a pledge for the reality of the next year's plant. But if we can give ideals over to Christ within us, then they are real seeds.

Norrköping 1914, GA 155

15 July

Increasingly an awareness will enter people's souls that we should not only say what we believe but test what we say against the objective facts. Christ will be the soul's teacher of reality, a teacher of our higher responsibility.

Norrköping 1914, GA 155

16 July

Humanity continually needs truths that cannot invariably be fully understood. To absorb truths means in fact not only to augment our knowledge, for truths as such contain life forces. By imbuing ourselves with truth we pervade the soul with an element of the world in the same way that we must continually pervade our body with air breathed in from outside us in order to live. This is why religious testaments contain deep truths, inner meaning, in a form people can often only discern at a much, much later time than when they were first revealed.

Norrköping 1914, GA 155

17 July

We learn to heal out of a true art, one that grows from an artistic vision and perception of the world.

Arnheim 1924, GA 319

18 July

But in future, when the spiritual renewal that also leads the intellectual up into the spiritual arrives at the end of the twentieth century, what nowadays only peers in as if through small windows must become a unity through the connection between the leaders of the School of Chartres and the leaders of Scholasticism. The people of the twentieth century must not waste the chance of this happening. But since everything depends on people's free will, whether it happens or not—that is, whether the parties thus allied with one another can descend to re-spiritualize culture—will also depend on whether the Anthroposophical Society is able to cultivate anthroposophy in the right, devoted way.

Arnheim 1924, GA 240

19 July

Michael is not the spirit who cultivates intellectuality; but everything he gives us as spirituality seeks to bring humanity insights in the form of ideas, the form of thoughts—but in the form of ideas and thoughts that encompass the spiritual.

Arnheim 1924, GA 240

20 July

One wishes that anthroposophists would awaken to others so that they know not only out of blind belief but out of real insight into the quality of the other why anthroposophy is all-encompassing and also includes what others think is the only outlook; that they know how anthroposophy broadens horizons because through it we can extend regions that others see only in a narrow scope.

Dornach 1923, GA 225

21 July

If with inward love we imbue ourselves with such things as I described in my book *Christianity as Mystical Fact*, where I tried to show how the contents of the ancient mysteries relate to the Mystery of Golgotha, then we come close to the initiation accomplished by the powers of wisdom.

Dornach 1923, GA 225

22 July

We would never have the capacity to surrender ourselves in love to another being or another process, as it were to enter fully into this other process, if the I did not truly depart from us every night so as to immerse itself in the things and processes of the outer cosmos. It does immerse itself in reality. And in slipping into us again in waking day-consciousness, through the ability that it has gained outside us it endows us inwardly with the power to love. This is what surfaces in the soul's deepest inwardness as threefold power: freedom, the life of memory, the power of love. Freedom is the inward archetype of the etheric body or body of formative forces. The power of memory is the inwardly appearing, dream-creating power of the astral body. Love is the inwardly appearing power of love that leads us to surrender to the outer world. It is because the human soul can participate in this threefold power that it can also permeate itself with cultural, spiritual life.

Dornach 1923, GA 225

23 July

If we rightly understood ourselves, then we would be able to do nothing other than look back upon our previous life.

Berlin 1918, GA 181

24 July

Much of the illness or disorder that lives in our soul will only find healing when we gain an interest in life that rests in truth, rather than avidly desiring fixed truths.

Berlin 1917, GA 176

25 July

It is not the role of spirit beings to exist where they ought not to. Most people wrongly regard the luciferic and ahrimanic elements as if these were something they wish to have nothing to do with. But it is completely mistaken to want to arrange life so that we have nothing to do with Lucifer and Ahriman. We must allow these beings validity in their own element and recognize that they only have harmful effects within elements to which they do not belong.

Dornach 1915, GA 162

26 July

Colour is the soul of nature and the whole cosmos, and by experiencing colour qualities we participate in this soul.

Dornach 1914, GA 291

27 July

If we do not ourselves develop our thinking we cannot.... approach the secrets of Jupiter through clairvoyance. You see, the secrets of Jupiter are such that they only reveal themselves in the form of thought. Only when we ourselves think can we approach the secrets of Jupiter, for it is the thinker of the universe. If we try to grasp some important enigma of existence in clear thinking, and fail to do so because of our human physical and etheric hindrances, especially due to astral hindrances, then the beings of Jupiter intervene and help us. The beings of Jupiter are helpers of humankind for developing our human wisdom.

Dornach 1923, GA 228

28 July

The true anthroposophist should know that it is important today for us to sympathetically observe and collaborate in the battle between Ahriman and Michael. Only where the spirituality that seeks to flow through the anthroposophic movement unites with other spiritual streams, will Michael find the impulses that reunite him with the intelligence that has become earthly, which really belongs to him.

Dornach 1924, GA 237

29 July

We must learn to paint out of colour. However poor our first attempts may be, it is our task to paint out of colour, to experience colour itself, detached from weight. In these things we must proceed consciously, also as artists.

Dornach 1923, GA 228

30 July

In sending humanity the Holy Spirit, Christ enabled us to raise ourselves from the intellectual realm in order to grasp the spirit.

Dornach 1922, GA 214

31 July

Consider this wonderful connection: the human being has a dual nature but apart from this fact, he bears both past and future already in his outward form. Reincarnation is tangibly present in our head, for what we find configured there is the result of our previous life. The head which we will bear in our next life will be the transformation of our present body.

Dornach 1916, GA 170

August

1 August

Really everyone in the anthroposophic movement should feel that they can only understand their karma if they see the prompting to read spiritually again in the 'book of nature' as one addressed to them personally. For the intervening period God made nature manifest and now we need to find its underlying spirit again.

Dornach 1924, GA 237

2 August

This is the great difficulty involved in forming ideas about economics. You see, the only way to form economic ideas is to regard them as something pictorial, metaphorical. Concepts will not allow you to grasp the economic process; you must grasp it in pictures. And this is something that scholars today find extremely uncomfortable—when anyone asks them to convert something from merely abstract schemas into a pictorial quality. But we will never be able to establish a real economic science without resorting to pictorial ideas, without becoming able to picture each economic process in dynamic and vivid detail. We need to know how any process in economic reality acts in specific detail when it is configured in one way or another.

Dornach 1922, GA 340

3 August

Whenever a closed sphere of economics exists such as the world economy, we ought to recognize that the only right form of economic management would be for all that is otherwise locked up in estate and property to vanish into spiritual institutions. It would have to disappear into spiritual institutions, and work like a gift. In other word, in our actual contemporary economics we need to try to answer this question: How should we buy and sell goods as economics understands it so that the nutritional values created in the purely material sphere disappear within the spiritual sphere? That is the big question.

Dornach 1922, GA 340

4 August

This is inscribed, really, in the karma of each and every anthroposophist: Become a person of initiative; and if, alongside your personal initiative, you encounter hindrances presented either by your body or by other factors that prevent you finding the centre of your being, observe that basically your sufferings and joys all depend on either finding or not finding this personal initiative.

Dornach 1924, GA 237

5 August

Humanity is on the way, in emerging from itself, gradually to transform spiritual reality into abstract concepts and ideas. In this respect humanity has already come a very long way, and the following may well await it. People could advance ever further in abstract, intellectual faculties, developing within themselves a kind of creed that says: Yes, we do experience the spiritual but this is a Fata Morgana, it has no weight, these are merely ideas. Human beings must find the ability again to fill these ideas with spiritual substance. They can do so by experiencing Christ at the same time as they pass into intellectual life. In other words, modern intellectualism must grow as one with Christ consciousness. As human beings we will inevitably fail to acknowledge anything at all unless we can find this Christ consciousness precisely upon the path of our developing intellectualism.

Dornach 1923, GA 214

6 August

Only if we understand the nature of objective thinking with its transparency, as this holds sway in lifeless nature, can we ascend to the other processes of thinking and beholding: to what pervades thinking with vision; with Imagination, Inspiration, Intuition.

Dornach 1922, GA 214

7 August

If you allow a wonderfully subtle poem like Goethe's 'Heather Rose' (*Heidenröslein*) to resonate in you, you can feel how the whole world is mysteriously contained in it, how world secrets are implanted in it. And so in fact the secrets of art gradually reveal themselves to us as we ascend from purely outward perception and feeling of things to an inward apprehension, from the microcosm to the macrocosm, and try gradually to acquaint ourselves with the secrets in our soul which, though hidden, are nevertheless active there.

Dornach 1915, GA 162

8 August

What unites the members of the Anthroposophical Society? They are united in the fact that they need to bring order into their karma!

Dornach 1924, GA 237

9 August

Let us awaken! This is something that should be regarded really as a kind of most intimate programme within the Anthroposophical Society. We would see people, a great many people go through life very differently, also anthroposophists, if they sought to be very, very awake, awake and fresh.

Dornach 1922, GA 214

10 August

If we now attempt as educators to introduce the least compulsion into what a person's own human nature wants; if we do not understand how to leave human nature freely to itself and offer only help in this, then we spoil the human being's organism for the whole of an earthly life.

Ilkley 1923, GA 307

11 August

Wherever we encounter the world, it is in reality spiritual and physical; nowhere is there something physical without a spiritual agency underlying it in some way. And there is nothing spiritual anywhere that leads to some kind of pointless and inactive existence simply to pass the time. Every spiritual reality that can be discovered becomes active, takes effect at some time or place, right into the physical.

Torquay 1924, GA 243

12 August

The number 12 contains the secret that we can absorb, assimilate an I. In as much as our senses have grown to be 12, 12 tranquil domains, they are the foundation of the I consciousness of the earth.

Dornach 1916, GA 170

13 August

There is not one world; there are as many worlds of space as the earth is composed of crystals. We gaze into an immeasurable vastness of worlds.

Torquay 1924, GA 243

14 August

Very few people today have any inkling ... of all that surrounds and encompasses the enigma of freedom. All initiation science must ... receive new light from the enigma of human freedom.

Dornach 1920, GA 199

15 August

The human being's truly aesthetic stance involves enlivening the sense organs in a particular way, and ensouling the life processes.

Dornach 1916, GA 170

16 August

One must be able to be an imaginative poet and, at the same time, not have to indulge this. At every moment of seeking insight one must be able also to create a play, a lyric poem, all kinds of things but also be capable of braking these imaginative flights and staying with the powers that otherwise only have significance in the most prosaic realms of life. Then, instead of entering imaginative fantasy we enter spiritual reality. For true spiritual vision an enormous amount depends upon this inner state of soul.

Torquay 1924, GA 243

17 August

The spirit is productive and creative. And above all, to work spiritually we must become creative. Upon the path of inner work, working our way into Imagination, we come close to the spirit, gradually enter into the spirit, into what is spiritual. We need only first feel the impotence of the intellectual and then we can find our way to the spirit.

Oxford 1922, GA 305

18 August

In the same way that Iphigenia is given as sacrifice to Artemis, but through this sacrifice becomes a priestess, so in the past centuries and millennia certain elements of our intellectual culture repeatedly had to be cleansed and purified, offered to the higher gods in a priestly, religious character so that this outward intellectual culture should not desiccate human hearts and souls. Thus Persephone is representative of the ancient clairvoyant culture, and Iphigenia the representative of the continuing sacrifice which our outward intellectualism must bring to deeper religious life.

Munich 1911, GA 129

19 August

The three golden rules of the art of teaching and education, which must inform the whole outlook of every teacher or educator, becoming the very life blood of their work—not in a merely intellectual way but imbuing the whole person—are these: Religious gratitude toward the world that reveals itself in the child, united with the awareness that the child presents a divine enigma that we must try to solve with our art of education; and a method of education practised with love, which enables children instinctively to educate themselves through us, so that we do not endanger their freedom. The latter must also be considered where it is the unconscious element of the power of organic growth.

Oxford 1922, GA 305

20 August

If a person begins to meditate, they undertake the only truly free action in human life… If we undertake a meditation every evening and morning so that we gradually learn to look into the supersensible world, this is something we can either do or not do. Nothing prevents or requires it. And experience also shows that most people who embark on meditative practice with the best of intentions soon cease to do this again. We are completely free in this. Meditation is an archetypally free act. And if we can keep faith with it, if we promise ourselves—not someone else but only ourselves—that we will keep faith with this practice, then this is already a huge power within the soul …

Oxford 1922, GA 305

21 August

Something very special and particular had to exist so that the spiritual presences so wonderfully revealed upon the ocean [at Tintagel] might flow in the right way into the mission, the task of King Arthur and his knights. Today the play of curling, foaming waves still continues, shimmering in the air, illumined by the sun, as if nature still everywhere brings forth spirit forms above this ocean, draws them from these crags. But to hold fast the spiritual presences in natural phenomena required not only a *single* person to perceive them. A whole group of people was needed, one of them feeling himself as a sun in their midst; and his 12 comrades were continually schooled so that their temperament, their sensibility, the whole expression of their being gave rise to a twelvefold quality: 12 individuals together configuring a whole like the signs of the zodiac around the sun… From this place, we can say, spreads Europe's civilization.

Torquay 1924, GA 240

22 August

Hitherto the tumultuous works of Schiller's youth have been renowned—*The Robbers, Fiesco, Love and Intrigue*. At most people have celebrated the sentimentalities of *Mary Stuart* or the really very externally dramatic scenes in *The Maid of Orleans* and the *Bride of Messina*. Today, though, we ought to begin studying his *Letters on the Aesthetic Education of Man*, in which he surpasses himself—with all his *Robbers*, with the whole of *Mary Stuart* and *Wallenstein*. We should begin not only studying these letters in their significance for humanity but allowing them to work upon us.

Dornach 1920, GA 199

23 August

It is because gods truly speak to us in genuine art that through art we will find the surest gateway for gradually engaging in what are known as the 'practical' aspects of life. Work is the foundation upon which our first principle can flourish: fraternal community, fraternal collaboration.

Munich 1909, GA 113

24 August

The way in which we relate to the outer world determines whether the very same being will be either nurturing or inhibiting, whether this same being can be either God or the devil for our soul organization.

Munich 1909, GA 113

25 August

Yesterday it was pointed out that the same beings who first approach us when we experience the astral realm in vision, and whom we then encounter when we progress further to illumination, when the astral becomes discernible to us, can either appear as good or evil depending on our own preparation. This shows the great transformative capacity of what, for our vision, does not descend as far as the physical plane but remains in regions of the higher worlds and descends only to the astral plane: it can transform from good into evil, from light into darkness.

Munich 1909, GA 113

26 August

It is part of our knowledge, our vision of Christ in the higher worlds, that we have prepared ourselves for this on earth!

Munich 1912, GA 138

27 August

A certain power—certainly not physical power but another, a spiritual power—lies in this Hegelian realm; it contains something that must be assimilated by every spiritual outlook. You see, spiritual science would inevitably become rachitic if it could not be permeated by the skeletal system of ideas that Hegel succeeded in wresting from Ahriman. We need this system of his. We must in a sense grow inwardly strong through engagement with it. We need this cool-headed deliberation if, in spiritual endeavour, we are not to lose our way in warmly nebulous mysticism.

Dornach 1920

28 August

We have meditation if we inwardly strengthen and awaken the soul, so that, as it were, we hear or see our thoughts. Meditation is a middle condition—neither thinking nor sense perception. It is a thinking that lives as vigorously in the soul as sense perception does; and it is a perception that perceives thoughts rather than outward things. Between the luciferic element of thought and the ahrimanic element of perception, our soul life unfolds in meditation as in the divine, spiritual element that bears within it only the progressive nature of world phenomena. The person who meditates, who lives in his thoughts so that they come to life in him in the same way that sense perceptions are alive, lives in the onward-flowing stream of the divine.

Munich 1913, GA 147

29 August

Trust is a golden word that in future must hold sway in social co-existence. Love for what we must do is the other golden word. And in future the actions undertaken out of universal human love will be the ones that will show themselves to be socially beneficial.

Oxford 1922, GA 305

30 August

Reality is something that arises from cognition. It is not something we must seek. Reality is something that we engender, in which we participate as we engender it; and the secret of the human being is this: that at birth a world surrounds us that is not full reality, so that we are born in order to complement what presents itself to us in outward sense appearance with something that only dawns within us.

Stuttgart 1921, GA 78

31 August

One knows what supersensible enquiry is once one has properly investigated the problem of freedom.

Stuttgart 1921, GA 78

September

1 September

Now it seems to me that however deeply one may have penetrated vision of spiritual worlds, it will not be possible to formulate these visions in a satisfactory way for our age if one is not able to connect spiritual vision with the scientific worldview of modern times.

Stuttgart 1921, GA 78

2 September

We have to be aware of a universal rule: rhythm replaces strength! This is an important esoteric principle. Nowadays people live in extremely arrhythmic ways, especially in their thoughts and actions. A person who only let the distractions of the outer world affect him, who only went along with them, would not be able to avoid this danger threatening his physical body as a result of the depletion of strength caused by esoteric development. This is why we must work to bring rhythm into our life. Naturally it's not possible to arrange our days so that each one is the same as the next. But there are some things we can do: we can carry out certain activities very regularly, and someone who undertakes esoteric development must do this.

Stuttgart 1906, GA 95

3 September

What is inward must be outwardly expressed through forms. Modern culture has lost such forms and must regain them. It must relearn how to outwardly express what lives within the soul. In the long term, form determines human co-existence. The wise people of old knew this, and that is why they held fast to the celebration of religious customs.

Stuttgart 1906, GA 95

4 September

The best books are those we must read and study again and again, those we do not immediately understand, that we must go through in thought sentence by sentence. When studying, it is not so much the content that matters but the way we approach it. By engaging with the great truths, such as planetary laws, we establish major trains of thought for ourselves and that is the important thing. There is also much egoism in saying, for instance, that you desire to read moral doctrines but nothing about planetary systems. True wisdom will engender moral life.

Stuttgart 1906, GA 95

5 September

To understand, for example, how something important for the whole of human evolution can come about through an individuality such as Abraham, you must attend very carefully and precisely to a principle, an important truth: that wherever an individuality is chosen to be a special instrument for humanity's evolution, a divine, spiritual being must directly intervene in this individuality.

Bern 1910, GA 123

6 September

If you regard soul life as being composed only of thinking, feeling and will, you cannot conceive of this soul life being protected beyond birth and death. Only when we progress from thinking, feeling and will to what is concealed within them, the astral human being, can we arrive at the human entity that is no longer bound to the physical body but can be conceived as integrated into the cosmos, into the soul-spiritual universe.

Dornach 1922, GA 215

7 September

In the era in which the human being achieved his full consciousness by virtue of thinking streaming downward as far as the physical organism and employing it, this thinking rejected the old, dreamy clairvoyance, which served as the foundation for an ancient cosmology and ancient forms of religious life. By this means human beings became able to develop objective science in the life of their physical organism between birth and death. At the same time they also gained the possibility of developing freedom. But nowadays we have arrived at a point where we must take the upward path again into the world of spirit, at the same time retaining our full consciousness: take the path into fully conscious Imagination, Inspiration and Intuition. In so doing we can complement our experiences of objective science and freedom with a new philosophy founded on knowledge of the supersensible world, a new cosmology, a new religious life. As revelations of a supersensible world, these can meet the needs of modern human beings just as the achievements of objective science, and of freedom, have met their needs for fully conscious awareness of the sensory world.

Dornach 1922, GA 215

8 September

To re-experience the state of soul of childhood in full consciousness is the prerequisite for a truly modern philosophy. And the prerequisite for modern cosmology is to fully consciously experience in the psyche a middle era of humanity's development, when the breathing process became a process of perception. Then also, the prerequisite for a conscious religion is to raise into modern awareness the soul state of primordial humanity—the earliest humanity on earth, when people still had a direct connections with the gods: to rekindle it in us and imbue it with full consciousness.

Dornach 1922, GA 215

9 September

In past eras, when a person wished to suppress the emotions, passions and egoisms of their astral body, they looked upward to higher regions and asked for strength from the heavenly realms. Then procedures were undertaken with them that deadened the harmful instincts of their astral body. But now the time came when, through the deed of Christ, human beings should themselves acquire in their I the power to rein in and tame the passions and emotions of their astral body. For this reason, the new truth about the astral body had to be proclaimed thus: blessed are they who are meek and gentle through their own powers, through the power of the I; for they will inherit the earth. This third Beatitude has profound meaning. It is worth examining in the light of what we have learned from spiritual science.

Bern 1910, GA 123

10 September

In our present age, the gods do not count on either themselves or their intentions being recognized by humankind. And much that only relatively recently was not left to human intentions has precisely now been included in them... If you wish to find the spirit, you have to look for it also where it becomes apparent in its great aberrations in cosmic evolution itself, as it outwardly unfolds, for this is where you can also find the beginnings of other things. It is the tragedy of modern civilization that people think that only human powers are at work everywhere, and that their source is solely to be found in life between birth and death. In fact, our world is everywhere pervaded by supersensible powers, spiritual potencies, that express themselves in the various things that happen.

Dornach 1920, GA 199

11 September

Now... the time is beginning when a person must feel: Pictures live in you from your pre-birth life that you must bring alive during your lifetime. You cannot do this with your I alone; it must work deeper into you, right into the astral body... If the world revolts today, it is the heavens that rebel; that is, the heavens which are restrained, constrained in human souls and which then do not manifest in their own form but in its opposite, becoming apparent in battle and blood instead of imaginations.

Dornach 1920, GA 199

12 September

Nowadays we cannot gain a right attitude to time through outward reflection but must have the ability to gain this right attitude through working inwardly on what is inward. We have after all entered the age of the consciousness soul, have left behind us the age of the rational or mind soul which was the Greco-Roman era. And this consciousness soul must increasingly develop in such a way that the beings of the higher hierarchies no longer work into us—for this would dull our consciousness—but instead we work our way upward to them. This must be part of our full, bright, clear day-consciousness: that we work our way upward to the beings of the higher hierarchies.

Berlin 1919, GA 193

13 September

How do we convey our I consciousness through death? Only the Mystery of Golgotha resolves this question. Humanity could never bear I consciousness through death if this consciousness, developed in the physical body, did not unite with Christ, who sustains it when it would otherwise melt away from the human soul along with the physical body..

Dornach 1922, GA 215

14 September

If we absorb the secret of the Mystery of Golgotha into our feeling life during our earthly existence, we thereby strengthen and empower our inner soul being so that, as we pass from the soul world into spirit land, it becomes potent enough to form a physical organism different from the one that must otherwise arise if no such impulse came from a renewed Christianity. You see, without this impulse, sickly organisms would arise in the future organization of the earth. Through a renewed Christianity we immerse ourselves in the impulse by means of which strong physical organisms can arise for the rest of earthly existence.

Dornach 1922, GA 215

15 September

If you dwell upon *Hamlet*, for example, you can feel how the whole vigour of Hector resides in him. But you can feel also that this strength cannot emerge in the post-Christian age, that it initially meets resistance—that here something has acted upon the soul that is only a beginning, whereas in ancient times an ending was implicit in the figures we encounter. ... We must inscribe this in our soul if we wish to understand what is meant at the very beginning of the Gospel of Mark: a 'beginning'. Yes, a beginning that shakes souls in their deepest being, that introduces an entirely new impulse into human evolution, a 'beginning of the Gospel'.

Basel 1912, GA 139

16 September

It is possible to imagine someone who is a complete non-believer and could only give artistic consideration to the Seven and Five at the end of the Old Testament, and then the Twelve at the beginning of the New Testament. If we consider this purely in compositional terms, we can still be captivated by the simplicity and artistic grandeur of the Bible, quite apart from the fact that the Twelve is composed of the five sons of Mattathias and the seven sons of the mother of the Maccabees. We need to learn to regard the Bible also as an artwork, and then we can gain a feeling for its grandeur, for the artistry embedded in it. And then we will gain a sense of what this embedded artistic element necessarily relates to.

Basel 1912, GA 139

17 September

In the body of Gautama Buddha lie the causes for all times, so that for all future ages human beings can inwardly develop the powers of the Eightfold Path, and this can become the possession of every person. The fact that the Buddha existed gave human beings the possibility of right thinking; and what will happen in this way until the whole of humanity has acquired the Eightfold Path will be thanks to the life of Buddha.

Basel 1909, GA 114

18 September

All of the teachings of Buddha have *one* characteristic in common; and this is why we find only one way of being in the pupils who directly belong to the Buddha. Similarly unified are the pupils of Socrates, since Socrates wishes for nothing other than to draw forth what lies within the human soul. Socrates in turn relates to his pupils in only a single way. But Christ Jesus stands in dual fashion before us: he relates in one way to his intimate pupils, and in another to the crowd. What is the reason for this?

Basel 1912, GA 139

19 September

What we encounter in Fichte, Schelling and Hegel, Christian thinkers of the greatest maturity, meets us in the pre-Christian era in Krishna. What is this Krishna manifestation in fact? It is something that could never recur again later, whose sublime nature must be seen as something that cannot be surpassed. Those who understand such things only gain an idea of the strength of the spiritual light that shines across to us from Krishna if they allow things connected with the culture from which he emerged to work upon them. We need only allow things to work upon us in the right way.

Basel 1912, GA 139

20 September

If we bring understanding to bear on the present moment, then we will also recognize that a fifth Gospel can be added to the other four. This evening, therefore, let us hear words expressing the mysteries of the macrocosm as complement to those of the microcosm. First of all in the Fifth Gospel will resound here the macrocosmic counterpart to the microcosmic prayer that was once proclaimed from the East toward the West. Here therefore may there reverberate, as a sign of understanding, the macrocosmic world prayer contained in the Fifth, primordially ancient Gospel, which is connected with the Moon and Jupiter just as the four Gospels are connected with the earth:

> AUM, amen!
> The evils prevail,
> witness of unleashing of egohood,
> incurred through others, selfhood-guilt,
> experience it in daily bread
> in which heaven's will does not prevail
> since man departed from your kingdom
> and forgot your names,
> you Fathers in the heavens.

The Lord's Prayer was a prayer given to humanity. In response to this microcosmic Lord's Prayer that was proclaimed from the East toward the West, the primordially ancient macrocosmic prayer now resounds. Thus it reverberates if, rightly understood by human souls, it sounds forth into the breadths of the cosmos and is given back in words formed out of the macrocosm. Let us take it with us, the macrocosmic Lord's Prayer, feeling that in doing so we begin to kindle understanding for the Gospel of knowledge, the Fifth Gospel.

Dornach 1913, GA 268

21 September

Altogether this is the secret concerning a great many things in the world of spirit: that the evil powers of the spiritual world can retain their power only for as long as one has no awareness of them, and no consciousness of them develops. Developing such consciousness is for certain adversarial or evil spiritual powers like daylight for ghosts—they flee from anyone's awareness of them.

Dornach 1923, GA 259

22 September

Beside water (and in the city this can of course also be replaced by other things, but only by exerting great effort; and what I will now say applies especially to things that come more or less by themselves), beside water, in vaporous mist, clairvoyant consciousness is particularly able to feel imaginations, everything imaginative in nature, and to employ what it has already achieved. On mountains, in thinner air, in different oxygen and nitrogen relationships, clairvoyant consciousness can more easily experience inspirations, allow new clairvoyant powers to emerge. And the occult powers find it hardest of all if one is at home, in one's own house, irrespective of whether one is alone or whether family members are there too.

Basel 1912, GA 139

23 September

In particular in the Gospel of Mark, less through the words themselves than the whole tone of the account, Christ emerges as a cosmic manifestation, as earthly and cosmic at once, and the Mystery of Golgotha as a fact simultaneously earthly and super-earthly. But something more is accentuated, and here we encounter a subtle artistry especially toward the end of the Mark Gospel. Emphasis is placed on the fact that a comic impulse shone into earthly affairs. It shone in.

Basel 1912, GA 139

24 September

Nowadays humanity needs gradually to appropriate the Eightfold Path in soul and spirit. It seems strange but it is true: everything that humanity achieved later in all its philosophical and moral doctrines is only a very weak beginning toward achieving what the Buddha first presented. However much people may admire all possible philosophies, however much they rave about Kantianism and other such things, all of it is trivial, is only elementary compared to the comprehensive laws of the Eightfold Path. And humanity can only slowly re-ascend to an understanding of what underlies the words of the Eightfold Path.

Basel 1909, GA 114

25 September

Precisely at the time when a number of people will have developed the teaching of the Eightfold Path out of themselves—in around three thousand years—the one who had become a Bodhisattva will then become Buddha, in the same way that his precursor became Buddha. Five to six centuries before Christ he was entrusted with his mission; and he will become a Buddha three thousand years after our era. This is the one known in Oriental teachings as the Maitreya Buddha. For the current Bodhisattva to become the Maitreya Buddha, a large number of people must have drawn forth the teaching of the Eightfold Path from their own hearts. There will then be sufficient numbers of people wise enough to be able to do so. And then the one who is at present Bodhisattva will bring a new power into the world.

Basel 1909, GA 114

26 September

There are three new powers that we seek to bring creatively to expression from spiritual sources: a visionary art once more, a perception of supersensible reality for the rebirth of soul, and of the spirit in that religion whose mood must emerge and shape itself from this art and this science…

Dornach 1920, GA 40

27 September

Life will only regain soul content when we can draw impulses from the cosmos and develop them in our soul and sensibility.

Vienna 1923, GA 223

28 September

The Michael powers do not want us human beings to implore them but to ally ourselves, join forces with them… People must really be able to have an experience of the spirit. They must be able to gain this experience of the spirit from mere thought, not, say, only from some kind of clairvoyance. It would be bad if every person had to become clairvoyant in order to develop this trust in the spirit.

Vienna 1923

29 September

Whereas, in the mid-nineteenth century people believed they could only become perfect through battle and strife, and so made battle into a great law of the world, they should learn now to develop the opposite of battle in their souls: love, which cannot sunder the happiness and wellbeing of the individual from the happiness and wellbeing of the other; which cannot regard the other as someone we must push aside for our own benefit. Once love is born in the soul then people will be able to discern creative love even in the outer world.

Berlin 1904, GA 53

30 September

What matters is this: that impulses such as the Michael impulse really always involve a person gaining supersensible insight into their connection not only with earthly circumstances but with cosmic ones; so that they learn to feel themselves not only as a citizen of the earth but as a citizen of the cosmos that is perceptible to them, whether they perceive it spiritually or in its physical reflection.

Vienna 1923, GA 223

October

1 October

Many will have this experience: sitting with a heavy heart in their room, weighed down by sorrow, not knowing how to go on, the door will open: the etheric Christ will appear and speak words of comfort to them. The living Christ will bring comfort to people! It may still sound incredible and yet it is true that when people sit together, knowing no way forward, even if they are gathered in larger groups, they will see the etheric Christ. He himself will be there, will give counsel, will speak his word in such gatherings. These times are certainly approaching; and this is the positive thing, the upbuilding, nurturing element that will intervene in humanity's evolution.

Basel 1911, GA 130

2 October

The death of Jesus of Nazareth was the birth of all-prevailing, cosmic love within the earthly sphere. This is more or less the first knowledge we can discern, decipher, in what we call the Fifth Gospel.

Kristiania (Oslo) 1913, GA 148

3 October

All that we can do in the way of enquiry into the world of spirit is to worthily prepare ourselves so that, when karma wishes it, when the world of spirit approaches us, we are not blind and deaf to this world. You see, we can prepare ourselves. But the world of spirit approaches us as an act or mercy or grace. This is how we should see it. We can therefore reply to the question of how someone can succeed in penetrating the spiritual world by saying: we prepare ourselves by virtue of everything that makes our thinking and feeling more supple and adroit, that schools our thinking, that makes our feelings finer, more devoted. And then we wait, wait! That is the golden word: to be able to wait in tranquillity of soul. The world of spirit cannot be conquered in any other way except by making ourselves worthy of it and then developing an expectant mood in soul tranquillity. That is the important thing.

Dornach 1914, GA 156

4 October

We can only come into relationship with a being of the world of spirit ... by enclosing it, enclosing it so that this encapsulation forms the cosmic consonants within which the being itself can announce itself to us in cosmic vowels. When such cosmic vowels can work together with the cosmic consonants that we have formed out of ourselves, then reading and hearing work together, and we can delve into a particular region of the world of spirit.

Dornach 1914, GA 156

5 October

What makes it possible to produce an 'ee' in ordinary human speech, is achieved in higher worlds by the feeling of soul that flows from devotion, surrender. Experience of this kind of surrender is one of the vowels of the higher worlds. We cannot perceive, read or hear anything in the higher worlds if we cannot, as it were, offer them this mood of soul—and then wait to hear what the beings of the higher worlds wish to communicate as we bring this soul mood toward them. Out of such moods of the soul, out of such ways of relating to the higher worlds, the vowel nature of the cosmos is composed.

Dornach 1914, GA 156

6 October

Books written about spiritual science are not usually read with sufficient attentiveness. They really are not, for if they had been then, after *Theosophy*, and *Knowledge of the Higher Worlds* and perhaps also *Occult Science*, all the lecture cycles should have been written or given by someone other than myself. Basically everything is already in these books... And if all that is contained in the four Mystery Plays were properly drawn from them, how much could then be written!

Dornach 1914, GA 156

7 October

Pure thinking, that is, developing primary, original activity, requires energy. The lightning of the will has to strike directly into thinking. But this lightning of the will also has to come from the utterly singular human individuality. People ought to try to have the courage to invoke this pure thinking, which also becomes pure will. And the latter gives rise to a new capacity: that of drawing directly forth from the human individuality moral impulses that must now be elaborated, that are not simply given as the old ones were. People should invoke intuitions [when realizing *The Philosophy of Freedom*] that are developed and elaborated! ... The nature of the divine lies precisely in invoking primary moral, spiritual intuitions. And once one has grasped the spiritual, then one can also unfold the powers which, taking this as their point of departure, allow us to encompass the spirit in further realms of cosmic existence.

Stuttgart 1922, GA 217

8 October

What is important ...is to seek the powers with which humanity's further evolution can unfold...Trust is one such power—trust between people. Just as, when we look into our own inner nature, we must invoke love for our ethical future, so, in regard to human relations, we must invoke trust. We must meet others by feeling them to be the riddle of the cosmos itself, walking cosmic riddles. Then we will certainly learn to develop feelings toward each and every person that draws trust from the very profoundest depths of our soul. Trust in a very tangible sense, individual trust, individually configured, is the hardest thing to help struggle its way forth from the human soul. And without an education, a cultural pedagogy oriented to trust, humanity's civilization will not progress. As we move toward the future, humanity will on the one hand have to feel the need to found all the life of society on trust, and on the other will need to acquaint itself with the tragedy that arises when people fail to allow trust to take up its rightful place in the human soul.

Stuttgart 1922, GA 217

9 October

From a human perspective it is simply part of life that, precisely in the realm of spirit and soul, we can be imbued inwardly by what I described yesterday as the medium of social co-existence: by trust. In this specific realm, this involves regarding what another says to us as a source, a fount, of distinct soul-spiritual experience.

Stuttgart 1922, GA 217

10 October

What needs to be disseminated with understanding are as many positive accounts as possible of how people actually develop, you might say positive accounts of the natural history of individual human development... This is needed above all: a study of life itself, the will for knowledge of life, not programmatic schemas. Theoretical programmes are the enemy of the fifth post-Atlantean cultural epoch.

Zurich 1916, GA 168

11 October

If for seven years one undertakes... *not* to do something that one has pursued as a favourite activity, and really keeps to this strictly, trying in quiet meditation to awaken the powers one has saved in this way, that would have been differently expended if one had continued the activity but now are available, it is relatively easy, at least to a high degree, to come to one's own perception of the things described in my *Occult Science*.

Bergen 1913, GA 140

12 October

Penetrating natural rhythms will be true science.

Dornach 1918, GA 184

13 October

If someone believes they can achieve the highest human ideal for earthly evolution upon a purely inner path of soul, through a kind of self-redemption, then a relationship with the objective Christ is not possible... The following insight is necessary for a person not only to find their way to Christ but also to ensure that their connection with the macrocosm does not rupture: If you commit error and sin these are objective, not subjective matters, and they cause something to happen in the outer world.

Karlsruhe 1911, GA 131

14 October

Anyone who, from the Mystery of Golgotha onward up to our own time, has sought a supersensible experience of the Christ event, has had to dwell on what—in the relevant lecture cycles which now really belong to the foundation of our spiritual-scientific work—are described as the seven stages of our Christian initiation: the washing of the feet, the scourging, the crowning with thorns, the mystical death, the burial, the Resurrection and the Ascension. Today let us examine what pupils can achieve if they allow this Christian initiation to work upon them.

Karlsruhe 1911, GA 131

15 October

In the same way that Gabriel passes nourishing powers to Raphael to transform them into healing powers, that is, passes on his golden vessel, and in the same way that Raphael passes his own golden vessel to Uriel, whereby the healing powers are transformed into powers of thought, so Michael is the one who receives these powers of thought from Uriel and, by the strength of cosmic iron of which his sword is forged, transforms these thought powers into the will, so that they become powers of movement in the human being.

Stuttgart 1923, GA 229

16 October

In our contemporary world we really ought to feel every spiritual endeavour to be inwardly mendacious if it does not seek a bridge to social efficacy.

Dornach 1920, 'The Art of Recitation and Declamation', 1928 edition.

17 October

Imagine for a moment a clairvoyant person who may perhaps have made very significant discoveries in the world of spirit through purely clairvoyant observations, but has failed to clothe these supersensible perceptions in a language available to the ordinary human sense of truth. Do you know what will happen to him or with him? After death all these discoveries are extinguished. After death there is only remaining value and significance in what has been converted, reformulated into a language that corresponds in any particular era to the language of healthy truth.

Berlin 1910, GA 124

18 October

What we usually absorb as history, what is regarded as academic history, should not be seen as the really important thing in humanity's evolution. We should regard it only as symptoms that flow upon the surface, through which we must look deeper into the reality of events; and then this reality can become discernible in humanity's development.

Dornach 1918, GA 185

19 October

If we characterize symptoms we should never try to be pedantically comprehensive but should always leave an unresolved residue, otherwise we get no further.

Dornach 1918, GA 185

20 October

If we regard this with all due seriousness, then we raise ourselves from a symptomatic observation of modern history to the following thought. Since the fifteenth century, things regarded as the human being's greatest achievement have entered human evolution: modern science, modern sociology, modern technology, modern industrial life, modern finance. But they bring death if they are not made fruitful by supersensible aspects. They are only capable of advancing humanity in the right direction if they are made fruitful by impulses of the supersensible. Then they are good.

Dornach 1918, GA 185

21 October

In evolution it must be so that what leads us upward to higher stages of evolution can also lead us into error… It is the mission of anger to prepare love … In wise dispensation the powers governing the world implanted the potential for anger into the astral body before a full consciousness of love can be developed, before love can come into its own in the soul in its full validity.

Berlin 1909, B81

22 October

There are ...two kinds of truth, which are two strictly separate realms of truth. We must distinguish between truths that arise for us through reflection on outward observations, and those that arise through primary thinking... What we conceive of in the latter sense has to be able to find its way into reality. The outcome of our primary thinking has to be able to come toward us in outward reality too, be confirmed there. The spiritual-scientific or anthroposophic truths are of this kind. They are ones that we cannot initially observe through our outward experiences.

Berlin 1909, GA 58

23 October

In reality there is only one esotericism, one occult truth. There cannot be an Eastern and a Western esotericism. This would be as clever as thinking you could distinguish an Eastern and Western mathematics. However, one or the other problem, one or the other question, can be better cultivated and explored in the East or the West, due to the distinctive qualities of the people there.

Berlin 1911, GA 133

24 October

Schiller's *Letters on the Aesthetic Education of Man* have been little understood in subsequent eras. I have often said how little people have studied them. Otherwise study of these 'Aesthetic Letters' would be a good way in to the content of my book *Knowledge of the Higher Worlds*. The letters by Schiller would be a good preparation for this. And similarly, Goethe's *Fairytale of the Green Snake and the Beautiful Lily* could prepare people for acquiring a mode of mental and spiritual apprehension that can arise not from mere reason or intellect but from deeper sources, and would then be able to really comprehend something like the lectures in *Towards Social Renewal*.

Dornach 1920, GA 2000

25 October

Growth *and* decline are something that must be consciously brought about in all life. Social structures cannot be built for eternity. Whoever develops social structures must have the courage to keep building further, anew, not to stand still. What has been built grows old, grows weak, must die, because something new must be built... Birth and death lived in people in a characteristic way in the fourth post-Atlantean epoch, that of the mind soul. Now, in the age of the consciousness soul, we must see it outwardly too, and must in turn develop something different within us. This is very important—to develop something different in turn.

Dornach 1918, GA 185

26 October

Since the beginning of the fifth post-Atlantean epoch, evil inclinations, tendencies to evil, lie in the subconscious of all people… There is no crime in the world from which any person in the world is immune in their subconscious, in so far as they belong to the fifth post-Atlantean epoch. They have the inclinations for it; but whether or not this tendency actually leads to an evil action depends on quite other circumstances than the inclination itself.

Dornach 1918, GA 185

27 October

The John Gospel has to be experienced. One must take its prologue as meditation and allow it to live within one. This is spiritual nourishment. We have to decide to live with its substance for five minutes every day. These words will open your eyes and ears of spirit. You will experience—in astral pictures—the magical power of these words, which are potencies.

Munich 1906, GA 94

28 October

The soul that has cultivated reverence will purify its dark sympathy and antipathy, its dark feelings of pleasure and displeasure into something we can call a feeling for beauty and goodness. The soul that has purified its will in the right way into reverent devotion will, if it has in the process also retained its self-feeling and self-awareness, cleanse the dark drives and instincts that otherwise pervade human desires and will impulses, gradually developing from these the inner impulses we call moral ideals. Reverence is the soul's self-education from dark drives and instincts, from life's desires and passions, to engender life's moral ideals. Reverence is something we sow in the soul as a seed; and it grows and blossoms.

Berlin 1909, GA 58

29 October

The child does not yet have character. The qualities, displayed in various activities, that are different from those of another child, are not yet character but individuality. The I has not yet taken its self-development in hand. It is still under the thumb of the sentient soul, still concealed and hidden. Until this I has becomes active, begins to play inwardly upon the strings of the instrument of the soul, the child is only an individuality, not a character. The characterological disposition only begins to emerge when the I starts to become aware of itself, initially dimly. Then, in the course of life, this self-education by the I increasingly arises.

Berlin 1909, B 81

30 October

The human being has to find his whole strength out of nothing.

Dornach 1920, GA 200

31 October

Whoever wishes to come to know the I in its own world has to be able to envision a world such as that of ancient Saturn... We have, as it were, to feel our surroundings completely saturated, imbued, with a quality that elicits in us horror, fear from all sides; and at the same time we must be able to overcome this fear through the inner stability and certainty of our being. Without these two inner moods, a shudder and fear at the infinite emptiness of existence, and the overcoming of this fear, we cannot get any sense at all of the ancient Saturn existence upon which our cosmic existence is founded.

Berlin 1911, GA 132

November

1 November

The outward instigation for the name of the Goetheanum seems to me to be that I said, some time ago in public lectures, that I, in my private opinion, would most like to call by this name the building where we intend to cultivate the spiritual outlook I represent. Last year already we debated this name, and this year some of our friends decided to support the idea of calling it the Goetheanum. As I said recently, for me there are a whole number of reasons for doing so—but they are not so easy to clothe in words.

Dornach 1918, GA 185

2 November

It is to the greatest degree harmful to someone's health if they are incapable of forgetting certain things.

Berlin 1908, GA 107

3 November

The more interest we have for an idea, the more we forget ourselves, with our egoism, in absorbing it, the better it will lodge itself in our memory. If we are unable to lose ourselves in relation to a thought, if will not easily be retained in our memory... The other thing we can endow a thought with is the power of judgement we inwardly possess. In other words, every thought is more easily remembered if absorbed with the power of soul judgement rather than simply being impressed on us.

Berlin 1910, GA 115

4 November

You will be able to shed a huge light, a lightning illumination on your whole life of soul if you make clear this one single thing: that all desires, wishes, interests, all phenomena of love and hatred, represent a stream in soul life that does not flow from the past into the future at all, but the reverse: from the future; it flows from the future back into the past.

Berlin 1910, GA 115

5 November

Already in the very early parts of Goethe's *Faust*, there lives so much of the wisdom necessary for understanding the world. This can be attributed to this singular unfolding of destiny, which really demonstrates how nature and the workings of the spirit are *one* in human development, how an illness is not just an outward physical matter but can have a spiritual significance.

Dornach 1916, GA 172

6 November

Thus a person really lives in the consciousness of deep sleep in relation to everything he engages with in a profession, for through this profession he is creating future worth—not through what he takes pleasure in about the profession but through what develops without him being able to attend to it. If someone makes a nail and keeps making nails, of course this won't give him a great deal of pleasure. But the nail itself has specific tasks. What happens through the nail is not something one worries further about. We don't trace the nail's future use after making it. But all of these things, that are wrapped in unconsciousness, in deep sleep, are fated to come back to life again in future.

Dornach 1916, GA 172

7 November

And someone who wishes to be clairvoyant will never say that he only wants to assimilate things he has previously checked and tested. He must be completely free from all self-seeking and must be able to retain an open expectancy for everything that approaches him from the world—which we cannot call by any other word than 'grace'. He expects everything from an illuminating grace. How, after all, does one acquire clairvoyant knowledge? Only by excluding everything that one has ever previously learned.

Berlin 1911, GA 132

8 November

It is because the spirit is to reveal itself out of human physical matter that this world today tends so greatly to materialism. It does not yet perceive the spirit, but rather the element out of which spirit is to come. This has given rise to the materialism which is primarily a Western product, but from the West has also flooded the Centre and is now expanding eastward... In the West, you see, spirit is a matter for the future, and the present gaze is initially turned to the body. But in human evolution everything is in flux: out of this bodily knowledge, this materialism, a spirit knowledge will eventually arise, albeit one that comes from a quite different direction and which will, above all, be conscious compared to the spiritualism of the ancient Orient.

Stuttgart 1920, GA 157

9 November

We must always seek the source of internal illnesses—those that are not caused by external injuries—in the metabolic system. If you want to observe illness in a fully rational way, you must start from the metabolic system. You must in fact interrogate every single phenomenon in the metabolic system by asking about its direction, where it is heading.

Dornach 1923, GA 230

10 November

From all sides it is as if the autumn crocuses were speaking to us, continually urging us to look upon our world of desires. 'O man,' they seem to say, 'consider how easily you can become a sinner.' The world of plants is indeed really the outward, natural reflection of human conscience. One can conceive of nothing more poetic than to picture this inner voice of conscience, emerging as if from a single point, as distributed across the most manifold forms of blossoms, speaking through the seasons to our soul in the most diverse ways. The plant world, if we know how to observe it in the right way, is the outspread mirror of conscience.

Dornach 1923, GA 230

11 November

If we do not only grasp but also think with our hand, then we trace our karma with this thinking hand. And with the feet especially: if we not only walk but think with our feet, we can trace our karma with especial clarity.

Dornach 1923, GA 230

12 November

You see, the world will increasingly ask human beings to work in specific and specialized ways. But the question will increasingly be what must also happen, apart from such specialization... In professional life it is necessary to develop conditions that have cosmic meaning, precisely by virtue of professional life detaching itself in a certain way from human interest.

Dornach 1916, GA 172

13 November

Why did the gods allow people to arise at all? It is because they could only develop in human beings capacities they could not otherwise have developed: the capacity to think, to picture something in thoughts, in a way that is bound up with discernment and distinctions. This capacity can only be developed upon our earth; it was never previously present and had to come about through the advent of human beings.

Stuttgart 1909, GA 117

14 November

Such preparation, connected with relinquishing wishes, desires and will impulses that arise in us, always leads to the greatest spiritual effects, let us say to magical effects.

Berlin 1911, GA 132

15 November

We must therefore strengthen soul life, strengthen it so that we approach what stands before us masked in dream within soul life. This can be done. We can do so fully consciously, in ways I described in *Knowledge of the Higher Worlds* and in other writings, through an exact and systematic meditative life, as it is called, which imitates dream life but not by creating artificial dreams. Instead we awaken to full consciousness in the soul what rises involuntarily in dream. We do this by accustoming ourselves to proceeding in the same way that dream involuntarily proceeds: by picturing things we know well, as symbols in inner meditation. Dream offers us symbolic chimeras of our own bodily nature. By contrast—since neither our own interiority nor nature provides us with symbols—we now practise picturing images in a rigorously systematic and symbolic way...

And in the same way we can imitate the other aspect of dream. We take events from our life, which may be many years apart. And we compile them according to perspectives so that one stands alongside another—yet not chaotically as in dream but according to perspectives which may also be drawn from imagination, and which we can survey in full consciousness. These do not force anything inwardly upon us but we ourselves form them inwardly. And so we gradually school ourselves to dwell within an inner life of soul; to dwell strongly in a soul life that arises entirely from inner activity.

The Hague 1923, GA 231

16 November

If you attend to ... the history of it, you will repeatedly hear that initiation science is cultivated in societies, in groups... How were such societies organized, and how will it be when knowledge of spiritual things once more comes to be integrated into civilization, when it is again called upon to imbue all areas of life, all areas of work? ... In societies of this kind things were arranged so that one person took over one area of knowledge, another a different one, by their own free decision. One person, say, focused their own spiritual enquiry upon the influence of the planets and stars on human life, while another studied the path of human life as it emerges from pre-earthly, spiritual existence into the earthly sphere. In this way people wished to be able to explore all the details of each area of knowledge...Thus each person was fully absorbed in the realm upon which they had particularly focused, and were glad to receive all other knowledge from their comrades...This is why a particular field of spiritual enquiry was assigned to one—or one singled it out for oneself—within which one relinquished the life-enhancing, enriching quality of receiving. On the other hand, one had this life-enhancing receptivity to what others gave. Something similar must again come about in future.

The Hague 1923, GA 231

17 November

Those who seek to delve consciously into the supersensible world and thus gain knowledge of it—or those who in other words wish to acquire capacities of 'ideal magic'—must do more than simply render their thoughts so inwardly intense that they can perceive a second existence in themselves as I described it. As well as this, they must liberate their will from its bondage to the physical body. We can only bring our will into movement in ordinary life by employing our legs, our arms, our organs of speech. The physical body is the foundation for our life of will. But we can do the following also, and this is something that those who seek to undertake spiritual research, and thus develop ideal magic in addition to exact clairvoyance, must do very systematically. They must for instance develop so strong a will that at a particular moment of their lives they say to themselves: you must shed a particular habit, and replace it with another that you incorporate into your soul.

London 1922, GA 218

18 November

The concepts prevalent today are often too lax in nature to disentangle the complex threads of life; you see, it is very often a matter of focusing on a certain point, then another, and then trying to relate these two points to each other, considering them both. If we take the right facts into account, we find points of light that can illumine a situation. And now you may ask how something like this can be done. Well, if you practise spiritual science in the right way, then through Imagination you will discover the points in life that you must bring together in vision so that life reveals itself to you… the important thing is to observe the world symptomatically.

Dornach 1916, GA 172

19 November

In the preceding period, from the child's seventh to fourteenth year, our former incarnation, now being fertilized by what occurs between death and rebirth, enters our bodily organization and makes us a reflection of our previous profession. In the following period, these impulses no longer work into us, no longer urge gestures upon us, but lead us toward our new profession.

Dornach 1916, GA 172

20 November

Whereas in ancient Greece people suffered the pain of copious questions, in modern times we are less exposed to this question-pain than to that of becoming spellbound by our prejudices, of having beside us a second body that contains our prejudices.

Dornach 1914, GA 158

21 November

It seems to me that Heinrich von Kleist described in the most significant terms what can live in a person—as you can read in the first section of *The Spiritual Guidance of Man and of Mankind.* He described what goes beyond us, what drives us and what we only later realize or recognize unless the thread of our life breaks off prematurely. Think of von Kleist's Penthesilea: there is so much more in her than she can encompass with her earthly consciousness. We could not grasp her whole singularity if we did not assume her soul to be infinitely broader than the little, narrow soul which she—albeit a figure of grandeur—encompasses with her earthly consciousness.

Berlin 1911, GA 132

22 November

The spirit of science must become personal again. The earth no longer gives its stimulus for this. For this we need the Christianization of science itself. If we imbue science with Christianity, we plant first seeds for the development of the spirit self... Libraries may have to shrink, and instead people will need to carry what can be found in libraries more in their souls. The spirit self can only proceed from this personalization of knowledge. This will not come about unless people acquaint themselves with what is now no longer earthly. You see, the earth has now passed the midpoint of its evolution. We have embarked upon a waning, dying process. Knowledge is dying in our libraries. It is dying also in our books, in these coffins of our knowledge. We must reintegrate knowledge into our personal being. We must carry it within us. Above all, renewal of the Mystery of Golgotha will help to do this; will help those with knowledge, those who are the disciples of the Golden King.

Stuttgart 1920, GA 127

23 November

First of all we perceive the supersensible in the immediate, sensory world, that of human beings, animals and plants. That is the path of Michael. And we pursue the same path further by finding the Christ impulse within this world, which we have perceived to be a supersensible one.

Dornach 1919, GA 194

24 November

The luciferic spirits live in the floods of light inlaying the clouds, just as the ahrimanic spirits live in the rising mists. Someone who can behold such things in conscious Imagination, allowing ordinary thinking to enter into the forms and colours of the continually changing clouds, allowing their thoughts to metamorphose, as it were, rather than keeping sharp contours; to transform, to expand then grow tenuous again, accompanying the forms of the clouds, their shapes and colours—then such a person can really begin to regard this play of colours upon the clouds, especially in the evening and morning sky, as a sea of colour in which luciferic figures are moving. And whereas melancholy moods are engendered in us at the sight of rising mists and vapours, in this case our thoughts, and with them also our whole sensibility, can learn to respire a greater freedom as we gaze upon this luciferic sea of flooding light. This is a special connection we can enter into with our surroundings; here, you see, we can raise ourselves to the feeling that our thinking is like a breathing in the light. We can feel thinking as a kind of breathing, but one occurring in the light. If you seek to experience this, you will better understand the passage in my Mystery Plays that speaks of the beings endowed with the power to breathe light. We can already gain a premonition of the nature of such beings in their respiration of light if we experience the kind of thing I have described. And in this way we discover how ahrimanic and luciferic qualities are also incorporated into the phenomena of outward nature.

Dornach 1923, GA 232

25 November

If you live with the John Gospel, you will awaken the power of vision within you. It is a seer book, written to school seership. If you live with it, sentence by sentence, the great and mighty outcome of this is that you come face to face, eye to eye, with Christ. It is not so easy to persuade people that they need to work their way through to the goal where the knowledge dawns on them that Christ is a reality. The John Gospel is the path that leads to Christ.

Basel 1907, GA 100

26 November

In relation to outward nature, nature precedes us and knowledge follows after; in relation to spiritual nature, knowledge—that is, what unfolds as a form of knowledge—comes first as preparation; sight comes after …In the same way that in science experience and knowledge arise from beholding, so in spiritual science, if human evolution is to advance, beholding of the world of spirit must develop from a knowledge of spiritual processes.

Berlin 1914, GA 64

27 November

We should not conflate a specific religious denomination with the being of Christ but connect *every* profession of faith with Christianity. If people could understand Christ in the way I have outlined, Christianity would spread everywhere across the globe. You see, the revelation of Christ and the revelation of Jesus are two different things… The Jesus revelation will also come to human beings in the right way. But they themselves must come to it. And they will do so once they have passed through a sufficient number of incarnations. Today already everyone is mature enough for the Christ revelation, to a certain degree.

Dornach 1916, GA 172

28 November

The brain will have the capacity to recall past lives on earth. But those today who have not ensured this in advance, by reflecting on themselves, will feel this capacity—which in them will be automatic—only as an inner nervousness—to use a contemporary expression; they will feel it as an inner deficiency.

Dornach 1919, GA 194

29 November

There are no effective social ideas within ordinary physical consciousness.

Dornach 1918, GA 186

30 November

This is what is necessary: no longer in future to distinguish, in abstract fashion, between what is material and what is spiritual but to seek the spirit within matter itself, so that it can simultaneously be described as the spiritual; and to perceive in what is spiritual the transition into materiality, and the way spirit works within matter…then we will no longer have abstract substance and abstract spirit, but interpenetrating spirit, soul and body. And that will be Michael culture.

Dornach 1919, GA 194

December

1 December

At Christmastide, the earth's windows open and archangels look through to see what human beings have been doing all year long.

Dornach 1922, GA 219

2 December

All the consonants in a language are really always variants of 12 archetypal ones. In Finnish, for instance, you find these 12 archetypal consonants preserved largely in their pure state: 11 are very clear, only the twelfth has become a little obscured...If we grasp these 12 archetypal consonants rightly—each can, at the same time, be represented by a form—and bring them together, they actually present us with the whole sculptural configuration of the human organism.

Dornach 1922

3 December

It is becoming increasingly dangerous for humanity to give itself up to the unconscious. Clear, bright appraisal, a regard for what actually exists, a sense of reality, is something humankind will increasingly need.

Dornach 1922

4 December

Today there are a number of souls who have come to the point of being very close to remembering their former incarnations, or the last incarnation at least. A whole number of people stand just outside the door, if you like, that is opening upon a comprehensive memory encompassing not only life between birth and death but at least the last of their preceding incarnations. When a number of people are reborn following this present incarnation, they will recall this one. It is a matter only of *how* they do so. Anthroposophic development should offer instigation and guidance for right remembering. From this perspective, we could characterize this anthroposophic movement by saying that it leads the human being to rightly grasp what we call the human I, the inmost aspect of human nature.

Munich 1909, GA 117

5 December

Within the world of *maya*, death is the only thing that shows its reality! All other phenomena are ones we must trace back to their reality; all other phenomena apparent in *maya* have their true nature underlying them... In reality only the human being dies, for he brings his individuality down as far as his physical body, within which he must be real during earth existence...But upon the physical plane we must take up our I consciousness. And without death we could not find this.

Berlin 1911, GA 132

6 December

Try to gain a sense of what it means to say that earthly processes are a shadow image of macrocosmic processes. Then you will have taken the first step gradually to be able to understand the Mark Gospel, one of the greatest documents of the world.

Berlin 1910, GA 124

7 December

In our modern culture it is also extremely difficult to comply with the demands of a life that will render the supersensible world accessible. Two preparatory conditions are entirely lacking in civilization today. The first is seclusion, called in esotericism a 'higher human solitude'; the second is overcoming the egoism that in our era has increased to its greatest degree though it remains largely unconscious to humanity. Lack of these two preconditions makes it more or less impossible to develop an inner life. Seclusion or spiritual solitude is so difficult nowadays because life increasingly distracts us, fragments us, or in other words requires our outward, sensory attention... The other hindrance is a kind of egoism, of which modern humanity usually takes no account, in relation to inner soul qualities... The preconditions for spiritual development include not seeking it out of egoism. If you seek it with egoism, you will not get very far. And yet our time is egoistic to its core. You can repeatedly hear people saying that all esoteric teachings are worthless for them unless they themselves can experience them. But if you start from this point of view, and do not shed it, you will find it very difficult indeed to succeed in any real higher development. You see, higher development requires the subtlest awareness of human community, so that it is of no importance whether I myself or another has this or that experience.

Berlin 1905, GA 54

8 December

Because the age of the consciousness soul is also at the same time the age of intellectualism, Germans, if they seek to enliven the consciousness soul in themselves in some way, must become intellectuals. This is why German people have primarily sought their relationship to the consciousness soul on the path of intellectualism, not that of instinctive life. And for this reason the tasks of the German people have only arrived with those who, to a degree, have taken their own self-education in hand.

Dornach 1918, GA 186

9 December

What one has acquired through imaginative perception, what one has thus beheld, fades after a few days. It only does not fade if one has brought it down to the level of ordinary understanding... Clairvoyance must exist only to find supersensible truths. The mission of the human being on earth is to comprehend supersensible truths by ordinary, healthy human reason. This is extraordinarily important.

Stuttgart 1923, GA 218

10 December

Basically we remain in the realm of ordinary life as long as we are making inward endeavours in meditation, as long as we are still involved in this effort. Only after exerting ourselves and allowing this exertion to work upon the soul, then suppressing this in turn and waiting in tranquillity, do spiritual-scientific results accrue.

Berlin 1915, GA 65

11 December

People who have endeavoured to be content in one period of their life gain this capacity to exert a harmonious effect on their environment in a subsequent period of the same life, as a karmic consequence. Simply through their way of being they have a beneficent effect on those around them. As we can invariably observe, benevolent people, people who have made efforts to be benevolent, gain the karmic consequence in a later period of their life that everything relating to them, and that they intend, is curiously successful.

Munich 1910, GA 125

12 December

There are 12 ways in which one can be initiated into the sun mysteries. Every initiation is in a sense a sun initiation, but each is nevertheless differently configured in relation to the other 11. Depending on whether a person has this or that mission for the whole of humanity, they receive a sun initiation whose powers, we can say, flow in as if the sun stood in a certain constellation, let us say the sign of Cancer. And this is different from receiving a sun initiation whose powers flow in as if the sun were standing in Libra. These are expressions for various specific types of initiation.

Munich 1910, GA 124

13 December

We can come to know a supersensible world, for we learn to discern error. In other words, we do not need to ascend into the supersensible world in an artificial way, for this world projects into us by sending us into error. And this has its effects. Yet this world we become acquainted with in consequence is not a good one. From another side, we must bring to it a good world, in a state of soul out of which error can only then act within the soul in the right way.

Berlin 1911, GA 115

14 December

If we consider the individuality of the prophet Elijah and his time, it is eminently apparent that the causative impulses working in human life by no means consist only in what is outwardly apparent and what external history reports. The most important processes at work in humanity are those occurring in human souls, which in turn work out of these souls to act further in the outer world and in other people. And though this can no longer happen in modern times, in ancient times such an individuality, known otherwise only by hearsay, could be one's simple, modest neighbour without anyone knowing this. The strongest, keenest powers of human evolution work in the most hidden way.

Berlin 1911, GA 61

15 December

Naturally there would be no supersensible knowledge on earth without clairvoyance, but even clairvoyants must transform into ordinary understanding what they perceive. However clairvoyant a person here on earth might be, however clearly they could behold the world of spirit, if they were too lazy to transform what they behold in the spiritual world into proper, logically comprehensible ideas, they would still be blind in the world of spirit after death.

Dornach 1922, GA 219

16 December

Assume for a moment that you read something and, simply by reading a scene that you find dramatically engrossing, you are moved to tears despite not being a sentimental person. Some great, good deed is described, it might be in a novel, and you are moved to tears. If you can observe yourself, you can discover that whole hosts of beings—which have such a subtle and intimately developed sense of shame that they wish to hide themselves from the sight of all other beings of the world of spirit— take refuge in your heart, altogether in your whole inner breast; seek protection from the other beings of the elemental worlds of spirit, especially from other warmth beings.

Dornach 1922, GA 219

17 December

Gabriel stands there in great consternation at any modern, educated person's content of ideas. Michael, who has an exceptional affinity with the powers of the sun, can at least interpolate his activity into the thoughts a person elaborates in so far as they give rise to impulses for free action. Michael can work his way into everything which I called 'pure thinking' in my book *Occult Science*. Such thinking must be the intrinsic impulse for the freedom of individual human will in the modern age. And Michael has a particular affinity with actions that spring from the impulse of love. This is why he is the messenger sent down by the gods to receive, in a sense, what is then led over from emancipated knowledge into spiritualized knowledge.

Dornach 1922, GA 219

18 December

People who wish to undergo esoteric development despite their immersion in daily, practical life, can attain their goal by virtue of the fact that Buddha works from Mars and not from the earth. In this way the powers for a healthy esoteric life derive from the activity of the Buddha... Rosicrucian esoteric development can be reconciled with every kind of situation and occupation in life.

Neuchâtel 1912, GA 130

19 December

In our actions we develop love by allowing our thoughts to shine into the element of will; we develop freedom in our thinking by allowing this will element to shine into our thoughts.

Dornach 1920, GA 202

20 December

In the forthcoming future, the gods will only have intentions for a human being where he himself also contributes to this. The human being must pass through inner battles that strengthen him... And what strikes us initially is the great battle that takes place between wisdom and love behind the scenes of the physical sense world. We are placed within this battle. For a long time it was unconscious; in future, we must place ourselves in ever more conscious ways into this battle waged in the world between wisdom and love. You see, our human existence should be what arises in the continual pendulum swing between wisdom on the one hand and love on the other. The nature of existence in the world partakes not of sleepy tranquillity but of rhythmic oscillations, the swinging back and forth of the pendulum.

Dornach 1918, GA 186

21 December

It is as if humanity, if it takes the opportunity to use these milestones of time as meditation material, can really become aware of its pure origins in the cosmic powers of the universe. Only by raising our gaze to the cosmic powers of the universe, and delving a little through Theosophia, through true spiritual wisdom, into the secrets of the universe, can we as humanity once again become mature enough to comprehend the higher level of the festival of the birth of Jesus once grasped by the Gnostics: this festival of the birth of Christ in the body of Jesus that should really be celebrated on 6 January. But—as if to enable us to immerse ourselves in the 12 universal powers of the cosmos—the 12 Holy Nights stand between the Christmas festival and the festival that should be celebrated on 6 January, which nowadays is that of the Three Kings, though it is really the festival that celebrates what I have described.

Berlin 1911, GA 127

22 December

Self-knowledge at the same time means knowledge of the gods, knowledge of the spirit, since every step leading inward is at the same time one that carries us into the world of spirit.

Dornach 1922, GA 219

23 December

The path to the Christmas mystery must be found anew. We must become as humble and pious through and in relation to nature as the shepherds were in their hearts. In our inner vision we must become as wise as the Magi became in their observation of the planets and stars in both space and time… Then we will find our way to the Christmas mystery.

Basel 1920, GA 202

24 December

What Osiris gives us to a higher degree through the Christ cannot be lost to us; but the figure who stands alongside Osiris for Christian understanding can be lost to us and has been lost: we have lost Isis, the mother of the Saviour, the divine wisdom Sophia… We do not lack Christ or perception of Christ, but we lack the Isis of Christ, the Sophia of Christ.

Dornach 1920, GA 202

25 December

Powers of genius we have in our later years we owe to the fact that we remained more childlike than those who have no, or fewer, such abilities. The preserving of childhood capacities into our later age equips us with particular creative inventiveness. The more we can preserve childlike capacities despite growing maturity, the more creatively active we will be.

Dornach 1920, GA 202

26 December

It really is very necessary for us to keep trying to bring together the stalwart, capable people in the world who can develop the skills to render anthroposophy truly practical. Recent centuries have not only somewhat dulled human knowledge but have in fact also suppressed human beings' truly practical abilities. People need to draw forth from the deepest realms of their being the necessary powers which everyone does in fact possess. We need a renewal from deep within of humanity's outward, practical capacities also. This birth is something we should aspire to: the birth of keen endeavour that seeks its way from within the human being, in contrast to the incapacity that we can encounter everywhere in the outer world today. This birth should hover before us in everything that we feel as Christmas mood.

Dornach 1920, GA 202

27 December

All true knowledge that wishes to have any prospect of engaging in any way with the riddles of the cosmos must emerge from the germ, the seed, of wonder… It is essential that before we start to think, before we even set any thoughts in motion, we have experienced the state of wonder…Thinking must originate … in wonder.

Hanover 1911, GA 134

28 December

You should not expect your thinking to give you knowledge of what is true. All you should expect initially is that your thinking educates you.

Hanover 1911, GA 134

29 December

As human beings are in the world today, subject to the luciferic influence, the relationship of the I to the astral body is not as it should be: the I is over-predominant... The I acquires the regular relationship necessary when a person, in wise, energetic and patient self-discipline, acquires qualities we have called wonder, reverence for what is discovered, the feeling of wise harmony with world phenomena, devotion and surrender.

Hanover 1911, GA 134

30 December

The ideal of modern culture must move toward regaining a kind of knowledge that can realize what Goethe already intimated, that can raise itself into art: not symbolic or allegorical art but real art, creative shaping of tones and words. At the same time such knowledge must also deepen into immediate religious experience. Only if we see this impulse as intrinsic to anthroposophic spiritual science do we understand the latter in its true nature.

Dornach 1922, GA 219

31 December

A future earth will only be able to arise if we are able to infuse this present earth with what it does not yet possess. The element that is not yet present by itself consists of active, effective human thoughts living and working in our organism, which the latter's state of balance makes independent of outward nature. If we realize these independent thoughts then we give the earth a future. But to do so we must first have them within us, these independent thoughts, for all thoughts in ordinary science have a dying quality, are reflections, are not realities. The thoughts we absorb from spiritual research are enlivened in Imagination, Inspiration, Intuition. If we assimilate them then they are configurations living an independent existence within earthly life…Thus spiritual knowledge is true communion, the beginning of a cosmic cultus fitting for contemporary humanity: a rite which can then grow as we become aware how we pervade our physical-mineral and our plant-like organism with our astral organism and our I organism; how, by bringing the spirit to life within us, we can implant the spirit into all that is dead and dying around us.

Dornach 1922, GA 219

In earthly working there comes close to me,
given in material life's reflection,
the heavenly beings of the stars:
within my will I see them loving move.

In watery life there is infused in me,
forming me in matter's strength and power,
the heavenly deeds of the stars:
within my feeling I see them wisely move.

Rudolf Steiner,
Dornach 31 December 1922

SOURCES

Volumes listed below from the Collected Works (CW) of Rudolf Steiner were originally published in German by Rudolf Steiner Verlag, Dornach. Published translations are listed in italics, whilst untranslated volumes are in quotation marks.

Quotations in this book begin with a capital letter, even where the original text does not start with the beginning of a sentence.

CW 40	*Truth-Wrought Words* (includes *Calendar of the Soul*)
CW 53	'The Origin and Goal of the Human Being'
CW 54	'Riddles of the World and Anthroposophy'
CW 55	*Supersensible Knowledge*
CW 57	'Where and How Does One Find the Spirit?'
CW 58	*Transforming the Soul, Vol. 1*
CW 59	*Transforming the Soul, Vol. 2*
CW 60/61	*Turning Points in Spiritual History*
CW 63	'Spiritual Science as a Treasure for Life'
CW 64	'From Destiny-Burdened Times'
CW 65	'Out of Central European Spiritual Life'
CW 66	'Spirit and Matter, Life and Death'
CW 74	*The Redemption of Thinking*
CW 78	*Fruits of Anthroposophy*
CW 83	*The Tension Between East and West*
CW 84	*The Aims of Anthroposophy*
CW 94	*An Esoteric Cosmology*
CW 95	*Founding a Science of the Spirit*

CW 97	*The Christian Mystery*
CW 99	*Rosicrucian Wisdom*
CW 100	*True Knowledge of the Christ*
CW 102	*Good and Evil Spirits*
CW 103	*The Gospel of St. John*
CW 104	*The Apocalypse of St. John*
CW 107	*Disease, Karma, and Healing*
CW 108	*'Answering the Questions of Life and the World through Anthroposophy'*
CW 109/111	*The Principle of Spiritual Economy*
CW 112	*The Gospel of St. John and Its Relation to the Other Gospels*
CW 113	*The East in the Light of the West*
CW 114	*According to Luke*
CW 115	*A Psychology of Body, Soul, and Spirit*
CW 116	*The Christ Impulse*
CW 117	*The Deeper Secrets of the Development of Humanity in Light of the Gospels*
CW 118	*The Second Coming of Christ*
CW 119	*Macrocosm and Microcosm*
CW 120	*Manifestations of Karma*
CW 121	*The Mission of Folk-Souls*
CW 123	*According to Mathew*
CW 124	*Background to the Gospel of Mark*
CW 125	*Paths and Goals of the Human Being*
CW 127	*The Mission of the New Spiritual Revelation*
CW 129	*Wonders of the World, Ordeals of the Soul, Revelations of the Spirit*
CW 130	*Esoteric Christianity*

CW 131	*From Jesus to Christ*
CW 132	*Inner Experiences of Evolution*
CW 133	*Earthly and Cosmic Man*
CW 134	*The World of the Senses and the World of the Spirit*
CW 135	*Reincarnation and Karma*
CW 136	*Spiritual Beings in the Heavenly Bodies and in the Kingdoms of Nature*
CW 138	*Initiation, Eternity and the Passing Moment*
CW 139	*The Gospel of St. Mark*
CW 140	*Life Between Death and Rebirth*
CW 144	*The Mysteries of the East and of Christianity*
CW 145	*The Effects of Esoteric Development*
CW 146	*The Bhagavad Gita and the West*
CW 147	*Secrets of the Threshold*
CW 148	*The Fifth Gospel*
CW 151	*Human and Cosmic Thought*
CW 152	*Approaching the Mystery of Golgotha*
CW 153	*The Inner Nature of Man*
CW 154	*The Presence of the Dead on the Spiritual Path*
CW 155	*Christ and the Human Soul.* Also *The Spiritual Foundation of Morality*
CW 156	*Inner Reading and Inner Hearing*
CW 157	*Destinies of Individuals and Nations*
CW 158	*Our Connection with the Elemental World*
CW 159	*'The Mystery of Death'*
CW 161	*Artistic Sensitivity as a Spiritual Approach to Knowing Life and the World*
CW 162	*'Questions of Art and Life in Light of Spiritual Science'*

CW 166	*Necessity and Freedom*
CW 167	*The Human Spirit*
CW 168	*The Connection between the Living and the Dead*
CW 169	*Toward Imagination*
CW 170	*The Riddle of Humanity*
CW 172	*The Karma of Vocation*
CW 174b	'The Spiritual Background of the First World War'
CW 175	*Building Stones for an Understanding of the Mystery of Golgotha*
CW 176	*The Karma of Materialism.* Also *Aspects of Human Evolution*
CW 181	*Dying Earth and Living Cosmos*
CW 184	*Eternal and Transient Elements in Human Life*
CW 185	*From Symptoms to Reality in Modern History*
CW 185a	'Historical-Developmental Foundations for Forming a Social Judgment'
CW 186	*The Challenge of the Times*
CW 188	'Goetheanism, a Transformation-Impulse and Resurrection-Thought'
CW 189	*Conscious Society*
CW 193	*Problems of Society*
CW 194	*Michael's Mission*
CW 196	*What is Necessary in these Urgent Times*
CW 197	*Polarities in the Evolution of Mankind*
CW 199	*Spiritual Science as a Foundation for Social Forms*
CW 200	*The New Spirituality and the Christ-Experience of the Twentieth Century*
CW 202	*Universal Spirituality and Human Physicality*

CW 203	'The Responsibility of Human Beings for the Development of the World'
CW 210	*Old and New Methods of Initiation*
CW 214	*The Mystery of the Trinity*
CW 215	*Philosophy, Cosmology, and Religion*
CW 217	*Becoming Michael's Companions*
CW 217a	*Youth and the Etheric Heart*
CW 218	*Spirit as Sculptor of the Human Organism*
CW 219	*Man and the World of Stars*
CW 220	*Awake! For the Sake of the Future*
CW 221	*Earthly Knowledge and Heavenly Wisdom*
CW 222	*The Driving Forces of Spiritual Powers*
CW 223	*The Cycle of the Year as Breathing Process of the Earth* and *Michaelmas and the Soul Forces of Man*
CW 224	'The Human Soul and its Connection with Divine-Spiritual Individualities'
CW 225	*Three Perspectives of Anthroposophy*
CW 226	*Man's Being, His Destiny, and World Evolution*
CW 228	*Initiation Science*
CW 229	'The Experiencing of the Course of the Year in Four Cosmic Imaginations'
CW 230	*Harmony of the Creative Word*
CW 231	*At Home in the Universe*
CW 232	*Mystery Centres*
CW 233a	*Rosicrucianism and the Modern Initiation*
CW 234	*Anthroposophy and the Inner Life*
CW 236	*Karmic Relationships, Vol. 2*
CW 237	*Karmic Relationships, Vol. 3*
CW 240	*Karmic Relationships, Vol. 6*

CW 243	*True and False Paths in Spiritual Research*
CW 257	*Awakening to Community*
CW 259	*'The Year of Destiny 1923 in the History of the Anthroposophical Society'*
CW 261	*Our Dead*
CW 266/3	*Esoteric Lessons 1913–1923*
CW 268	*Mantric Sayings*
CW 271	*'Art and Knowledge of Art'*
CW 275	*Art as Seen in the Light of Mystery Wisdom*
CW 277	*'Eurythmy: The Revelation of the Speaking Soul'*
CW 283	*The Nature of Music and the Experience of Tone in the Human Being*
CW 284	*Rosicrucianism Renewed*
CW 291	*Colour*
CW 304a	*Waldorf Education and Anthroposophy II*
CW 305	*The Spiritual Ground of Education*
CW 306	*The Child's Changing Consciousness*
CW 307	*A Modern Art of Education*
CW 314	*Physiology and Healing*
CW 319	*The Healing Process*
CW 340/341	*Rethinking Economics*

Verse on p. vi: CW 40
Verse on p. 404: CW 219

Books are available from Rudolf Steiner Press, UK www.rudolfsteinerpress.com or SteinerBooks, USA www.steinerbooks.org

A note from Rudolf Steiner Press

We are an independent publisher and registered charity (non-profit organisation) dedicated to making available the work of Rudolf Steiner in English translation. We care a great deal about the content of our books and have hundreds of titles available – as printed books, ebooks and in audio formats.

As a publisher devoted to anthroposophy...

- We continually commission translations of previously unpublished works by Rudolf Steiner and invest in re-translating, editing and improving our editions.

- We are committed to making anthroposophy available to all by publishing introductory books as well as contemporary research.

- Our new print editions and ebooks are carefully checked and proofread for accuracy, and converted into all formats for all platforms.

- Our translations are officially authorised by Rudolf Steiner's estate in Dornach, Switzerland, to whom we pay royalties on sales, thus assisting their critical work.

So, look out for Rudolf Steiner Press as a mark of quality and support us today by buying our books, or contact us should you wish to sponsor specific titles or to support the charity with a gift or legacy.

office@rudolfsteinerpress.com
Join our e-mailing list at www.rudolfsteinerpress.com

RUDOLF STEINER PRESS